C000005282

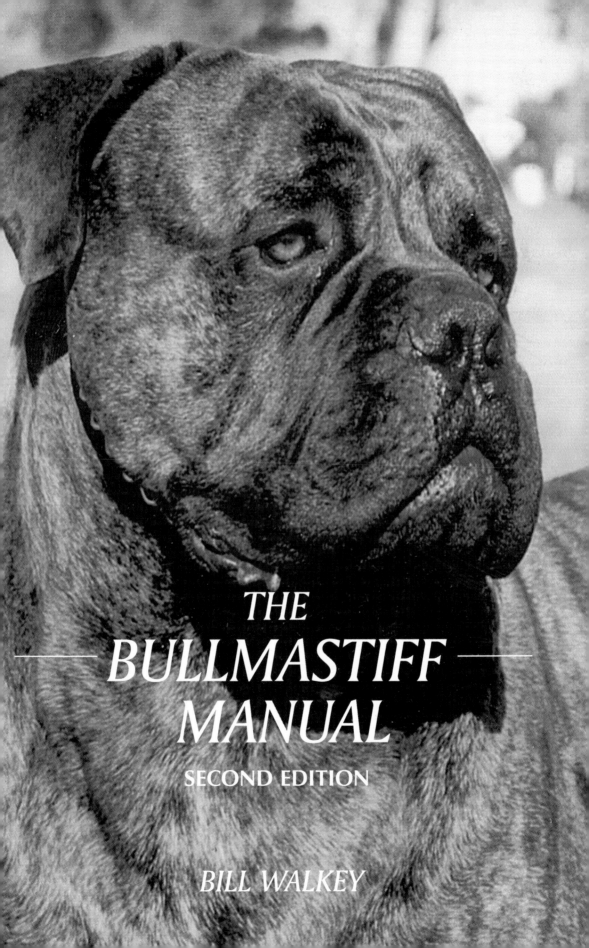

THE
BULLMASTIFF
MANUAL

SECOND EDITION

BILL WALKEY

t.f.h.

KINGDOM

Front cover: Aust Ch Forestguard Hannibal, owned by Brad Hansen of New South Wales.
Back cover: Ch Dox Fast Freddy of Shady Oak OFA, owned by Dr John and Susan Crawford.
Title page: Aust Ch Forestguard Hannibal.
Contents page: Ch Mc'Kimsey's Red Highland Rogue.

CONTENTS

PREFACE

It occurred to me many years ago that the uniqueness of the Bullmastiff was lost in the generality of other bull breeds and often, incorrectly, it was grouped with them in respect to psychology, temperament and disposition.

This love affair with the breed took me to many Bullmastiff kennels in the United States, Canada Finland and Britain, and I asked questions wherever I went. What I learned over these many years, and the experience gained from it, is the basis of the information found in this book. There is a look that says 'This is a Bullmastiff'; a look you will never forget, that stirs you from within. If that look is not there, it is not a good Bullmastiff...or maybe is another breed.

My hope is the same as that of Mrs Doris Mullin (Mulorna Kennels), in that I hope I can leave the breed just a little bit better than I found it and trust that posterity will do the same.

Bill Walkey

FOREWORD

It is a privilege to write the foreword to this new edition of *The Bullmastiff Manual*. I have long been an admirer of this noble and stalwart breed.

The Bullmastiff's history dates back to the 1860s when the breed was developed in England to serve as a companion and estate guard dog. Their purpose was to discourage the common practice of poaching on the numerous large English estates. Their strength and apparent ferocity proved very successful in combating the poacher problem. Referred to as the gamekeeper's night dog, the Bullmastiff would intercept poachers and its very strength and weight would hold the intruder down on the ground until its master arrived on the scene. This is an important point for fanciers to keep in mind. Do remember that the breed standard calls for: a symmetrical animal, showing great strength, powerfully built, but active. The dog is fearless yet docile, has endurance and alertness.

Bill Walkey (Shayla) has been involved with Bullmastiffs for many years. He has a proven record as a successful breeder, having bred and raised numerous top show and specialty winning animals. It is extremely important that breed books be written by experienced and successful breeders. They have travelled the hard roads, encountered the many hurdles and obstacles on the way and completed a difficult course in order to attain their goals. Their valued advice on such matters of breeding, selecting, developing, rearing and maintaining healthy, valuable breed specimens cannot be underestimated. One important signpost of a good breeder is that they let other breeders and fanciers have the results of their experience and sound breeding practices. Bill Walkey is such an individual as the dog show results prove. It is a wonderful gift when an individual finds a goal in life to which their efforts never cease. Bill's whole life revolves around this breed, its unique character, its historical background and the importance of maintaining and preserving correct breed type.

Bullmastiffs (60% Mastiff and 40% Bulldog) have become increasingly popular. To raise one to healthy maturity requires the knowledge that this book contains. Their breed history makes fascinating reading. May this book be enjoyed by all dog lovers, fanciers, exhibitors and judges. A treat is in store for you in the pages that follow – read on, learn, enjoy and always keep the flag flying high for our noble and loyal Bullmastiffs!

Leslie B Rogers, Langley, BC, Canada
CKC registered all-breeds judge.

Mindy Stouer's Ch Blazin's Bull Bodine (Blazin's Studz McKenzie ex Ch Blazin's Irish Mist).

INTRODUCTION

The names Bullmastiff, Bull and Mastiff, Bandog, Tiedog and Gamekeeper's Night Dog have created an identity confusion of the breed known today as the Bullmastiff. It is one of the few dogs that was not adopted by Royalty and hence has not enjoyed the promotional publicity enjoyed by such breeds.

Owing to this, its origins, purposes and history have become a little obscure over time and lost in the annals of history. In the 1930s, breed historians such as Eric Makins and Arthur Craven did their best to acquaint the public with the breed of that time.

This book provides background, methods and a 'how-to' for novices and first-time owners, plus a host of information for the long-time fancier, in a comprehensive format to supplement the true fancier's library.

Korik's Virtual Reality pictured at 12 weeks old (Ch Blackslate's Irving Frye ex Am Can Ch Windridge Absolute Reality TT). Owned and bred by Deneen Newport and Scott Fraser.

CHAPTER ONE

Introduction to the Breed

Can Ch Khalsa's K.O. Kasmir.

Aust Ch Soloshel Miss Molly with Kimbullad Princeothieves (brindle), Kimbullad The Regarder (red dog towards rear of dam) and Kimbullad Chaudron (red bitch near dam's head). Owned by Mr and Mrs Harris.

A Bullmastiff playing the part of 'Keeper', Emily Brönte's dog.

Any room for humans? The gang on holiday in Devon.

So you have decided to add a special member to your family but are not sure which breed to choose. Well, let me tell you about a special dog: the Bullmastiff. He is large: at 0.75m (2ft) high at the shoulder and 58kg (130lb) in weight, he is an ominous deterrent to intruders. To his family, however, he is a big, soft, loving pet. He is gentle with his loved ones and does not take up as much room in the house as his appearance first suggests. He is quiet, not usually barking unless there is a problem he cannot investigate; then he barks to warn you of the problem.

The Bullmastiff's coat is waterproof, so he can thrive when kept outside in a sheltered kennel. The breed was originally developed to guard estates, so your garden must be fenced to give him his (your) estate boundaries; the neighbours may not appreciate your dog claiming their gardens as his private property! A Bullmastiff is too heavy to jump over fences; he jumps against them. To avoid a collapsed fence it is a good idea to have a rail about 1.5m (5ft) off the ground on your fence for him to jump against.

The Bullmastiff will be naturally defensive of his own territory, so gates at all points of access should be secure. There is nothing more upsetting to an unsuspecting acquaintance entering your property for a friendly visit than to find a Bullmastiff coming to investigate him at full speed. On the positive side, the Bullmastiff is a knock-down-and-pin dog, not a biter, so your guest may feel a little indignant but will come to no harm as long as he does not retaliate. If he does, the dog will stand no nonsense.

You should not consider buying a Bullmastiff if you live in a flat or apartment, as it will be difficult for you to give the dog the necessary exercise. Running your dog loose in the local park is not advisable unless you have complete and total control over him. Remember, the dog was bred to be a fearless protector and therefore dominant. No amount of spoiling or pampering will affect his genetic make-up.

Since the breed is relatively unknown, many people out with their dogs will not know a Bullmastiff or his temperament, often mistaking him for a Boxer cross or some form of Mastiff. Unaware of the defensive nature of the Bullmastiff, they may allow their dogs to be totally uninhibited and free. Flare-ups will occur if a dog running loose in the park challenges your Bullmastiff. Your Bullmastiff should not be criticised for being antagonistic to male dogs challenging him as this is a natural reaction. However, considering the size discrepancy, a defensive snap by the Bullmastiff could be fatal to the interloper. Bullmastiffs will normally tolerate strange female dogs as long as they are submissive. This also applies to neutered males.

Shayla's Brok, aged two, with puppy and baby.

The dog is a soft, loving pet to his family.

For a Bullmastiff owner it is best to avoid confrontation. It is sometimes very aggravating while trying to exercise your dog to encounter so many owners who allow their dogs to run freely, exercising no control over them whatsoever. However, this does not reduce the responsibility of the Bullmastiff owner to avoid such confrontations. Any irresponsible attitude by a Bullmastiff owner is detrimental to the owner, the dog, the breed, and the public. Although the dog is a soft, loving pet to his family, any challenge by a foolish or misguided dog or a malevolent owner will cause an aggressive response from your Bullmastiff – and you will be held responsible!

Family? What is the dog's family? It is anyone you choose in your close family relationship: friends, parents, the postman, all those you regard as familiar characters, the people with whom you feel safe and secure. Your Bullmastiff will never guard against his 'family', so consider this fact when you introduce your dog to other people. Other 'non-family' associates will be treated as outsiders.

The Bullmastiff is not a breed that approaches each new person with growls and snarls of rejection, but is a confident dog who knows his own worth. Under your guidance he will admit strangers into your home, but he will always keep an eye on them.

The key is the tone of your voice. If it is relaxed, so is his manner. If your voice is agitated or raised in anger or excitement he will be wary. In such a situation it would be very unwise for someone to move towards you quickly, even in jest, as your dog will step in to protect you.

British breed judge Mr H E Price of the Lombardy affix says that one of the first questions a prospective newcomer to the breed will ask is, 'What are they like with children?' His answer is as follows:

> *Personally I firmly believe that children should not be left alone with any dog, large or small. Inevitably, accidents will happen. We have had one or two such incidents in Great Britain that the press and television reporters have treated sensationally. Much of what has been said is inaccurate. In my experience, covering a great many years and a fair number of dogs, there is no safer dog than a Bullmastiff with children! For some reason hard to define they will tolerate much from a young child to which they would most certainly object from an adult, and they make excellent guard dogs for 'their' children.*
>
> *There will be the odd rogue in any breed but, looking below the surface, you can usually find good reason for bad behaviour. Many people let their dogs get out of control in the sadly mistaken belief that this is kindness. All dogs of any breed, particularly the large guarding breeds, should be taught obedience from an early age together with respect for and tolerance of children. Similarly, parents must educate their children to realise a dog is not a toy to be played with. A little common sense would prevent most accidents. If a dog is known to be aggressive, special care must be taken where children are involved.*

Can Am Ch Shayla's Keeper Alargh Ddu, the only Bullmastiff to win both the Canadian and the American National Speciality Shows. Bred by the author.

Ch Blazin's Bull Bodine, aged 2^1/2 years. Owned by Mindy Stouer of Pennsylvania.

Left: Bullmaster Sweet Melody (16 months). Centre: Bullmaster Miss Revenge (7 months). Right: Bullmaster Sweet Success (16 months). Owned and bred by Bullmaster Kennels, Victoria, Australia. Photo: Animal Pics

Ch Starvelley Makoush at 20 months. Owned by Mr and Mrs D B Ceronio.

Remember: you are the controller. Watch your voice and consider your responsibility to your dog and your guests. What do you think would happen if your dog was lying quietly in the front hall and your child, who had been playing outside with a friend, suddenly burst through the front door, shrieking in excitement and hotly pursued by his pal? Think about it. These are some of the responsibilities an adult owner must consider when owning this large, impressive, powerful yet soft and gentle dog. Which part of the dog's disposition you see depends on you.

When you bring home a cute little eight-week-old pup, his soft, beseeching eyes will tug at your heartstrings. Until one year of age he will be gaining approximately 4.5kg (10lb) each month. At nine months this amounts to a large 41kg (90lb) bundle of fun who is still a puppy at heart and who still thinks he can leap on to your lap. He may be big and heavy, but he is still a baby. This exuberant and large baby will have to be convinced not to jump playfully onto the Pekingese next door or its elderly owner.

Minding the child – or minding the Smarties!

Bullmaster Indiana (Weilhana Barossa Baron ex Ch Nightwatch Lady Nikita).
Owned and bred by Bullmaster Kennels.

You may be used to the size of your pet, but those around you may not be so keen.

Bullmastiffs usually live no longer than 10 years. Problems associated with this breed may include Osteochondritis Dissecans (OCD), Entropion, Gastric Torsion (Bloat) and Hip Dysplasia (HD) (see chapter 9 for more detailed information). Although most dogs are not bothered by these

Ch Mc'Kimsey's Red Highland Rogue aged three years old.

Can Am Ch Shayla's Karleigh Alargh Ddu, bred and co-owned by the author.

Bulltyron Zulu Dawn, owned by Scott and Narelle Cook of New South Wales, Australia.

Bullmaster Sweet Melody.

Ch Nightbeauty Benson Lee. Bred by I R and M G Hemming.

problems, some are, so it is best to be aware of them when considering a Bullmastiff as part of your household.

One thing is sure: if you do allow a Bullmastiff to be your friend, you will be converted for life and he will give you many years of loyalty, love, protection, warmth and affection.

Ch Blazin's Hillbully Jethro.

CHAPTER TWO

Origin And Development

One of Mrs D Daniell-Jenkins' first dogs, Grange Tiger, with her daughter Mary, around 1940.

Did you ever wonder where the Bullmastiff breed came from? Many myths, stories and tales have drifted down through time, some from supposed authorities, but very few attempt to discuss the breed's origins in depth and detail.

British Origins

The antiquity of the English Mastiff has been doubted by many who believe the breed as we know it today to be a relatively new one. This is true, but the same can be said of any current breed: the dog we see today is the form presently known to us. What must not be overlooked in our tunnel vision of pure-bred pedigrees is that all our accepted breeds have evolved through the centuries from some medieval or earlier ancestor. The word that confuses most people is mastiff. People suppose the word means massive, when the derivation has nothing to do with size but comes from an old English phrase 'masse thefe' meaning to master a thief – in other words, a thief-catcher. Unlike today's meaning of 'thief', a medieval thief sometimes had four legs, not just two. Dogs in medieval times were not kept for fancy; they had to earn their daily portion of food. Early dogs, by natural selection against the elements and predators, had to be big and strong. Early man harnessed the dog's natural territorial capabilities to guard flocks and herds against wolves and other dangerous predators. Pictures of dogs resembling mastiffs have been seen on the walls of Egyptian tombs 3000 years old.

The Old English Mastiff was the descendant of the Celtic war dog that fought alongside his master in 55BC and terrified the Roman soldiers during the punitive invasion of Britain by Julius Caesar. Had it not been for the fact that the elephant the Romans had brought with them trumpeted in fear and scared the Celts, the Romans would probably have lost the day. The strength and size of these dogs so impressed them that they took some home to Rome to fight in their arenas.

The early Briton referred to his canine companion as a mastiff. His counterpart on the European continent referred to his equivalent as a dogue (dog). When Norman French was imposed on Britain after William the Conqueror succeeded at the battle of Hastings in 1066, the different references to the same animal caused misunderstanding. The European masters believed the Anglo Saxon was calling his dogue a massive (mastiff) dog.

Engraving of Duke of Hamilton with Bulldog, 1790.

Before William's arrival, not only did the Anglo Saxons keep dogs for personal protection, but their Anglo Saxon lords made it illegal to do otherwise. In each village the King's representative, the Regarder, made sure that for every two villeins (peasants) there was one mastiff. The reasoning behind this was that the villagers' dogs would be used to keep down the number of wild animals that might prey on the King's deer. This put the onus of deer protection on the villagers, although they were not allowed to sample the fruits of their labour.

The Regarder carried with him a mastiff gauge. Through living under the protection of man for so long, smaller mastiffs that would otherwise have disappeared through natural selection had survived. If these smaller mastiffs could squeeze through the gauge, they were considered harmless as deer runners. Those mastiffs too large for the gauge had to have three toes from one of the front feet removed to prevent their running the King's deer. This was done by taking a chisel and a mallet and removing the toes, known as expeditation.

The size discrepancy between these two mastiffs was used to the benefit of Britons down through the ages. The smaller dog became the Bulldog, the larger one the Old English, or Giant, Mastiff. Many centuries passed in their development, but both types were still descended from the same common animal.

Bull-baiting was outlawed by Queen Victoria in 1835, but the law was ignored for about 10 years. Therefore by the mid-19th century a big, tough, heavy, aggressive Bulldog was still being bred: a prime animal for holding a bull immobile by its top lip, but not really big enough to overcome a man.

A mastiff gauge.

The Giant Mastiff, on the other hand, was big and strong but did not have the tenacity and aggression of the Bulldog. The Mastiff's fighting and aggressive temperament had been bred out over the years to produce a large, impressive dog that was tied in the daytime, but allowed to roam at night.

At the beginning of the 19th century some residual state of the feudal system was still operating in Great Britain. The aristocrats had land, wealth, big houses and estates; the common working man had very little, and usually not enough food to feed his hungry family. Regardless of the law or the consequences of breaking it, men were ready to take risks to provide for their starving families by poaching game from the big estate, especially if the estate owner had an abundance of game and little use for it except as recreational hunting.

A typical old time Mastiff.

To prevent depletion of their game stock in this way, the estate owners employed gamekeepers. As the 19th century progressed poachers began to take quite a toll on the estate's game resources, and the gamekeepers were hard pressed to keep up with the increasing number of infractions.

Poachers had learned that there was safety in numbers, often poaching in gangs so that they hopelessly outnumbered the lone gamekeeper. It was not uncommon for gamekeepers to be found dead or badly wounded; the poachers had no intention of being caught, as the penalty for poaching was death or deportation. Against odds like this poachers considered the murder of a gamekeeper in the dark of night well worth the risk.

Life was very uncertain for the gamekeepers and even more frustrating for the estate owners. They knew that local villagers, who by day touched their caps and bid them 'Good day', were the same villains who marauded in gangs at night to steal their game.

Gamekeepers had always had dogs of the terrier type to control vermin, or lurcher-type dogs to control rabbits and hares. Although well suited for this specialised work, they were most ineffective as personal guards. The gamekeepers needed a dog that was rough and tough and could take the physical abuse of kicking, punching, even blows from a club, or anything a desperate man in fear of being caught might inflict. The dog needed to be quiet and able to lie unnoticed and unseen in a thicket until ordered to take his man. To this end a brindle dog was preferred. In the early morning or late evening when most poaching was done, the brindle's stripes allowed him to blend into the background. Many gamekeepers bluffed the presence of a dog when in fact there was none, as it was well known to poachers that the dog's colour rendered him practically invisible. The fawn colour appeared as more fawn mastiffs were introduced in some areas, and red, with the secret interbreeding with the Dogue de Bordeaux. This dog resembles a coarse version of the earlier type of Bullmastiff, making it relatively easy to introduce the red colour by secret breeding, secret because the early breeders wanted their dogs to have the status of pure bred rather than cross bred animals. The first fancier to exhibit red Bullmastiffs was excused from the ring and asked to take his 'long legged red Bulldogs' with him.

The dog needed to be able to communicate silently with his master to alert him if someone was moving nearby, giving the element of surprise to the gamekeeper. The Bullmastiff communicated with the gamekeeper by ear movement and wrinkling its brow when someone was approaching, and this warning was all the gamekeeper needed.

The need for the dog to go instantly on command from a lying position to a fast, forward charge demanded well-developed thighs and hindquarters, especially in the area between the stifle and hock known as the second thigh. This muscular second thigh is the primary source of power, permitting the dog to vault forwards from a lying position to a full charge.

Various mastiff types had been tried, but none seemed to suit the need completely. Some gamekeepers introduced European mastiffs they had seen at the popular London shows into their breeding program. In his search for the night dog he so desperately needed the gamekeeper interbred such dogs as the Great Dane, St Bernard, Dogue de Bordeaux, Dalmatian, or any other breed he felt might help him. These strange mixtures of gamekeepers' night dogs were a motley crowd. Depending on the criteria of individual gamekeepers, dogs were developed along individual lines, but none quite came up to expectations.

Dogue de Bordeaux, source of the red colour in Bullmastiffs.

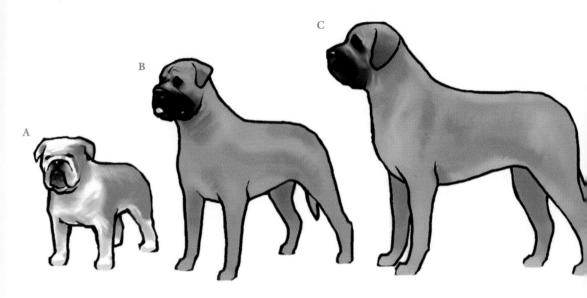

Forty percent from the old-type Bulldog (A) and sixty percent from the Giant Mastiff (C) went into the making of the Bullmastiff (B).

Results were not convincing until the appearance of the straight cross of the Bulldog and the Giant Mastiff (see diagram above), referred to in different circles as Bandog, Night Dog, Tie Dog and the Bull-and-Mastiff. This straight cross produced excellent results. The dog was a simple cross of the Bulldog of the time (a much heavier and larger version of the animal we know today, referred to in history books as the Butcher's Dog) and the Old English Giant Mastiff.

It seems ironic that the two types of medieval dogs used to protect against thieves should join up many centuries later to catch poachers. It was a common understanding among pioneer Bullmastiff breeders that by the time deliberate crosses of the two types of dogs had been made to produce the Bull and Mastiff, some shrewd gamekeepers had already recognised the natural cross of these two breeds and were using them.

Depending on the lineage and source of this new found cross, the temperament was often unpredictable. Some were too large and lethargic, others were too aggressive and injured their quarry. The gamekeeper needed a correct balance of these two breeds, large enough to knock a man down and hold him until he could be apprehended, and yet small enough to be quick, tenacious and aggressive enough to pursue a man on command with vigour and enthusiasm. The gamekeeper did not want the quarry mauled or injured; he simply wanted to turn him over to the Bailiff for imprisonment or deportation, getting him well away from his estate.

One fancier quick to recognise the usefulness of this dog for both estate guarding and police work was a man by the name of S E Moseley, of Hamil, Burslem, Staffordshire. He calculated that a correct blending of 60% Mastiff and 40% Bulldog would solve the criteria needed by gamekeepers and law enforcement officers alike. He therefore took a straight cross of 50% Bulldog and 50% Mastiff (the Bull and Mastiff) and bred it with a 100% Mastiff, which resulted in a litter of puppies which were 75% Mastiff and 25% Bulldog. This animal he bred to a 50:50 type to obtain a dog 62.5% Mastiff and 37.5% Bulldog. The closer percentage of 60:40 was adjusted by selectively breeding to other lines where genetics had produced a slightly different mix.

Local influence of type was affected by interpretation to produce bullier dogs in the north of England, more mastiff type in the south. However, in 1924, a consensus of the early breeders produced the first Kennel Club Standard, and the Bullmastiff (one word) was born.

Mr Moseley first showed one of his dogs on 6 August 1925 at Bagnall, Staffordshire, under judge R T Baines, when one class was scheduled for the breed. The dog, Farcroft Fidelity (facing page), was the first dog of the breed ever shown as a Bullmastiff. Ironically in true Bullmastiff manner Farcroft Fidelity's dam, Farcroft Faithful, died protecting her owner from poachers on the Yorkshire Moors. Her owner carried her two miles and buried her where the family could see her grave from the house.

In 1926 in one class of 10 entries at Crufts, the judge, Sam Graham, awarded first place to Mr Moseley's Farcroft Fidelity, second to Mr B A Morriss' Stand Aside, a dog sired by Farcroft Fidelity, and third to Mr W H Aldred's Topsy's Brutus.

The following year (1927) there were eight classes with 47 entries. The judge, Mr J W Marples, awarded the first place in dogs to Farcroft Fidelity, and the first place in bitches to Farcroft Silvo.

The breed progressed until in 1928 The Kennel Club granted Challenge Certificates (CCs) for the breed at four shows: Crufts, Manchester, The Kennel Club, and Birmingham. The judge, Mr H P Brown, awarded the first CCs to the breed at the Crufts show; the dog CC to Tiger Prince, owned by Vic Smith of Pridzor Kennels, the bitch CC to Mr Moseley's Farcroft Silvo.

Farcroft Silvo went on to be the first-ever champion in the breed and during her lifetime earned herself 14 CCs. In Britain, three CCs are needed before a dog becomes a champion; Farcroft Silvo acquired her 3rd CC, and therefore her title, under judge R S Whitson. Prior to this, on 28 February 1928 at Newcastle, Farcroft Silvo was the first Bullmastiff to go Best in Show (BIS) (any variety or sex). This was truly a magnificent distinction for a dog whose breed had only recently gained recognition.

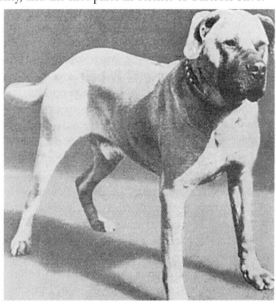

Farcroft Fidelity.

Moseley was an enthusiastic advocate of the breed and his kennel name of Farcroft was soon to be seen wherever he could introduce it. In fact it is questionable whether the Bullmastiff would have become so popular had it not been for his persistence in promoting the breed; he was convinced it would make an excellent police dog and was successful in its introduction in many areas. It is only fitting that a female from his line, Farcroft Silvo, was the first champion and BIS.

Other formative kennels who made significant contributions to the early breed were Bulmas, Oldwell, Harbex, Bulstaff, Kelwall, Mulorna, Rhodenhurst, Pridzor (see page 21), Marbette, and many, many others too numerous to list. More information about British champion dogs and kennels can be found in Chapter 10.

In the years after the recognition of the breed, hard work by the founder breeders produced an impressive guard dog, admired all over the world and imported into many countries where men no longer needed to guard their pheasants or deer, but their personal property.

North America – And Beyond

When Bullmastiffs first made their appearance in North America there was more concern by those interested in the breed to establish good lines and specimens rather than nationalistic pride or competition. The American Kennel Club (AKC) recognised the Bullmastiff as a separate breed in 1933, the Canadian Kennel Club (CKC) in 1939. The first Bullmastiff to be registered in America was a fawn bitch by the name of Fascination of Felons Fear (AKC 914895 Farcroft Felons Frayeur ex Farcroft Fortitude) owned by Mr John Cross Jr of New York. Fascination was bred by the breed's founder, Mr S E Moseley, and was whelped on 18 March 1933. Mr Cross obviously liked what he saw because he bought many other dogs from Mr Moseley in successive years. On 1 October 1934 Mr Cross registered two other dogs under his 'Felons Fear' kennel name, a fawn bitch by the name of Fondant of Felons Fear (AKC 950570 Bowdercourt Penner ex Farcroft Floranda), whelped 22 January 1934, and a fawn dog, Founder of Felons Fear (AKC 950569 Farcroft Finality ex Farcroft Fealty), whelped 10 July 1932. Mr Cross registered his first home bred dog on 1 May 1935, a fawn bitch by the name of Felons Fear Forest Fawn (AKC 986283 Founder of Felons Fear ex Fascination of Felons Fear), whelped 9 January 1935: a proud day for Mr Cross.

Mr Cross purchased numerous dogs from England, many of them from Mr Moseley, but the English import that became the first Bullmastiff champion both for Mr Cross and the United States was a fawn bitch by the name of Jeanette of Brooklands of Felons Fear. She was bred by Mr T Pennington from England out of his bitch Bubbles and sired by Roger of the Fenns, whelped 1 April 1934, and registered by Mr Cross in the United States on 1 March 1936. Although this new champion's lines were reinforced by the original pioneer lines of Farcroft and Pridzor, it fell to Mr Pennington to supply the USA with its first champion. As a matter of record, the Brookland affix was the earlier name of the kennel later known as Rhodenhurst. In England if a kennel fails to pay the annual fee needed to sustain the affix, the name lapses. Such an oversight caused the loss of Brookland, which was quickly replaced by the soon-to-be-famous Rhodenhurst name.

For the statisticians, the first fawn Bullmastiff registered in the USA was Fascination of Felons Fear (mentioned above), whelped 18 March 1933 and registered 1 March 1934. The first red was a dog called Neil (AKC A49-997 Simba ex Freya of Germains), whelped 25 November 1933 and registered 1 March 1936. The first brindle was a dog used repeatedly by the early breeders called Bluff (AKC A161-678 Mackwyn Excelsior ex Woodacre Stormer), whelped 12 October 1935 and registered 1 July 1937.

As stock was so limited these dogs were obviously imports from Britain. At this time the Bullmastiff Breeders of North America based in Albuquerque, New Mexico united the Bullmastiff fanciers of both Canada and the United States as there was not a separate club for each country. The American breed club, The American Bullmastiff Association, held its first sanctioned show in 1956, and was elected as an AKC member club in 1964. In 1950, the Honourable Bullmastiff Fanciers of Canada was formed, but later changed its name to the current Bullmastiff Fanciers of Canada.

Bluff, the American brindle dog registered by Mr C H Turner on 1 July 1937, was not only formative to the American fancy but foundation to the original Canadian stock. Bluff and Rhodenhurst Ruby (A134-4980) were sold to Daniel J Moran of Ponca City, Oklahoma, who bred them and produced a litter of seven on 24 June 1937. Mr Moran sold a red-fawn bitch from this litter to Mrs Edna M Bowman of Nevada, Missouri. This was Farvale Sentinel (AKC A194-929) who was bred back to her father, Bluff, and whelped on 30 April 1939. One of the litter, a dark brindle dog (AKC A375-817) was registered under the name Pride of Elgin and was the first Canadian registered Bullmastiff. Some confusion occurs in the early records at this point as the dog is shown as sold to Mr Byron W Parker of Aylmer, Ontario, Canada in the AKC records of 1939, but registered in the CKC records of 1941 as the first Bullmastiff under Mrs Bowman's name. Whoever owned him, he was the first in Canada (CKC 158726).

About the same time as this piece of history was made, Mr Victor Dane of Tarzana, California, was breeding Fairhazel Jenny (AKC A396-762) to Toby of Le Tasyll (AKC A396-759), both of whom he had imported, and on 28 February 1940 produced a fine sized litter among which was a red, female puppy whom Mr Dane called Harbex Duchess. She was sold to Mr Byron W Parker of Aylmer, Ontario, the same Mr Parker who owned the American-bred Pride of Elgin. Duchess had the distinction of being the second registered Bullmastiff in Canada alongside her mate.

The resultant litter from Mr Parker's two dogs whelped on 18 March 1942, giving him six dogs and two bitches. The most famous member of this litter was a dog puppy sold to Mr and Mrs H W Mellish of Victoria, British Columbia, who registered him under their affix as Heatherbelle Emperor (CKC 183810) in 1945 and listed him as slate fawn with a black mask. In 1946, at the age of four, this dog earned the distinction of being the first Canadian champion.

The need for more stock was obvious and the number of dogs exported from Britain to the USA continued to increase until the early 1960s.

In Canada there were more arrivals to the west coast than to the east from such kennels as Mulorna (Mullin), Stanfell (Higginson), Rhodenhurst (Pearce), Bulstaff (Short), Le Tasyll (Nash), Bulmas (Leeke), Buttonoak (Terry) and Harbex (Warren), all of which provided fine examples of the breed to the Canadian fancier.

Mrs Nash's Springwell Major went to enhance the guard team of dogs used by the De Beer diamond company of South Africa. The Mau Mau uprising in the early 1950s saw more Bullmastiffs arrive in South Africa to protect the property owners.

Douglas Fairbanks became the proud owner of Trixie of Le Tasyll, and Jean Drapeau, Mayor of Montreal, employed Robertstead's Duke Ferdinand (Duc) as a body guard.

Some of the better-known dogs that arrived in North America at this time were Hector (209687 Milford of Mulorna ex Model of Mulorna), Pioneer (209688 Rhodian ex Meg of Mulorna) and Sylvia of Mulorna (209686 Rhodian ex Clover of Mulorna), imported in 1946 by the air ace Paul Burden of New Brunswick. Unfortunately Mr Burden's kennels fell victim to a disastrous fire. Mrs E Lawton, who had worked for Mrs Doris Mullin in England, moved to Canada in 1947 and took with her two dogs bred by Mrs Mullin, Rhodian Junior (241902 Rhodian ex Meg of Mulorna) and Mimico Marionette (241903 Rhodian ex Sheila of Mulorna). This same year Mrs Daniell-Jenkins of Picton, Ontario, imported Robin of the Rouge (239166 Robin Hood of Le Tasyll ex Betty of Stanfell) from Mrs D J Nash's Le Tasyll kennels.

In September 1951, the first Bullmastiff specialty held in Canada by the newly-formed Honourable Bullmastiff Fanciers of Canada, sponsored by the Progressive Kennel Club of Canada, was held at Dixie, Ontario. There Robin of the Rouge attained a BIS, the first ever Bullmastiff to do that in North America.

In 1952, Mrs Daniell-Jenkins imported Bulstaff Tapestry (307643 Chips of Harbex ex Tess of Halebridge), a fawn brindle, and in 1953 Artist of Buttonoak (331876 Pridzor's Reward ex Bimbi of Bulmas), a male fawn. To the west coast of Canada went the famous Rhodenhurst Monarch (386819 Rhodenhurst Marksman ex Rhodenhurst Jeanie), a male fawn bred by Mr E L Spruce and imported by Mr W F Dyer of New Westminster, British Columbia.

It is interesting to note that this stream of dogs continued to the west coast of Canada whereas in the USA the tendency was

Robin of the Rouge, winner of the first Canadian Specialty, 1951.
Photo: Ted Jenkins.

25

towards the east coast. By 1962, five out of the seven litters registered in Canada were from British Columbia. The accumulation of dogs on the west coast was to have a profound effect on the Bullmastiff population of the western states.

From the fine stock of Lyn and Dave Rosenstock (Regalstock) and Geri and Dave Powell (Blackmist) came the founding dogs for many of the western American kennels. This interaction on the west coast between neighbouring fanciers complemented the earlier assistance of the American kennels such as Felons Fear had given to their Canadian counterparts. Many of the now well-known US kennels such as Teddersbelle, Bulbrook, Shastid and Tauralan owe their roots to the early work of such kennels as the Regalstock and Blackmist.

On the east coast of the USA Mr Cross was doing a fine job of bolstering the breed with his importing and careful breeding. Another importer was Mr D McVicar who bought many dogs from Mr Moseley as guards for the Rockefeller estate. These dogs were registered under the Pocantico prefix which can still be found behind many lines today.

Mr Cross and his fellow fanciers were breeding many fine litters and increasing the number of Bullmastiffs both in the USA and in eastern Canada while in the west the Canadians were assisting the western USA fanciers, a good example of international co-operation where political boundaries account for nothing in concerns of breed importance. East and west eventually met with a melding of qualities, ideas and types. The tremendous distance of the width of the North American continent is not without its problems of communication and breed type inconsistency. However, as

the early North American pioneers such as Mr Cross and Mr Parker overcame the lack of stock and the small gene pool, so the modern breeders strive to improve type variation and temperament.

Photography, video cameras and frozen semen all assist in today's world to shorten the distances of east and west. To epitomise the place of Bullmastiffs in North American history, Mr Ed Schwartz sponsored a four feet high statue of a Bullmastiff which was unveiled in October 1989 in Philadelphia. Truly a great tribute to the breed!

The pedigrees of the early dogs mentioned in this chapter can be seen in the appendix at the back of the book.

Development of the Breed in Great Britain

The following detailed account of the development of the Bullmastiff in Great Britain is kindly contributed by Mr H E Price of the Lombardy affix, a well-respected breed judge.

A Bullmastiff statue in Philadelphia (sponsored by Mr E Schwartz).

It is generally accepted today that the keeper's night guard was the forerunner of the breed, though it probably bore no resemblance or relationship to the dog we know as the Bullmastiff. It was bred for one purpose only: to protect its master, a trait that is still found in some of today's dogs. This dog would have been made up of anything available, mostly the old bull-baiting dog of that era, and it would have been a capable killer. What it did to its victim mattered very little; a poacher's life was very cheap. Many put forward the idea that this was simply a 'holding' dog but, in my opinion, those that put this idea forward are seeking to justify poor mouths in their stock.

Around the end of the last century, many knowledgeable writers referred to the Bull-and-Mastiff and the Bull/Mastiff Cross, and even the term 'Bullmastiff' that we use today was not unknown. We can therefore safely assume that this was when the first serious attempt to create our breed was made. In the early 1900s the Bullmastiff was becoming established, often being used as a guard dog.

The first world war devastated the breed, setting progress back for years. In the early 1920s Frank Moseley came on the scene. His Farcroft Bullmastiffs must be behind every modern Bullmastiff. His aim was to popularise and standardise the breed type and this was the beginning of pedigree Bullmastiffs. Thanks to his efforts The Kennel Club recognised the breed in 1924 and the breed steadily gained popularity. Several celebrities owned Bullmastiffs: HRH The Duke of Gloucester, Sir Gordon Richards and Rafael Sabatini, the famous author, among others. Vic Smith, another founder of the breed, went down in history when he took the very first Dog Challenge Certificate (CC).

The Second World War saw the end of this period of development of the Bullmastiff. Many went out of the breed, leaving just a handful of dedicated breeders, fortunately with a good nucleus of stock. It was then that the Bullmastiff as we know it today was created, mainly through Cyril Leeke's Bulmas and Mr Higginson's Stanfell kennels. These established the type and head style we know today, very different from the long-muzzled, snipey pre-war dogs.

I have been asked to write on the various lines we have today but I do not think we have any clear and definite unrelated lines. There cannot be a Bullmastiff in this country that does not have Ch Roger of the Fenns (a pre-war dog) somewhere in its pedigree or, coming nearer to our time, Ch Branch of Bulmas or Ch Ambassador of Buttonoak. These were so well used that they must figure in the background of all today's Bullmastiffs. It therefore follows that all of today's lines have the same background. What we have actually seen over the years is a series of well-known stud dogs that have dominated the breed.

I came into the breed in 1950 when the Bulmas kennel was without equal; almost every champion was sired by a Bulmas dog. The greatest of them all was my all-time favourite, the one and only Ch Branch of Bulmas, sire of many champions. Cyril Leeke's emigration to the USA virtually ended the Bulmas line in this country. He took his best with him, returning a few years later with nothing, never to take up the breed again.

Ch Zeela of Oldwell (b 1980).

Following on, Mr and Mrs Terry's Buttonoak kennel came to the fore, and they created their own line. They had enormous success with Ch Bimbi of Bulmas, one of the finest bitches of her day. Swatchway Amethyst was the dam of the extensively-used Ch Ambassador of Buttonoak; Ambassador Son, Anthony and Alaro were all household names in the breed. Regrettably this kennel came to a sudden end; some of the young ones were sold off and, I believe, the older ones put down. However, it is certain that Ch Ambassador left his mark on the breed forever. Type and colour was the legacy he left, and many of today's notable kennels are based on this dog.

In the early 1950s several kennels were just emerging and establishing their own lines. Perhaps the most influential was the Oldwell kennel of Harry and Beryl Collias (see page 23). This was based on Buttonoak and Marbette stock and dominated the breed for more than three decades. Harry's policy was to use only Oldwell dogs over a wide range of bitches. Since he was able to keep a huge kennel his policy paid off handsomely, and he made up champions too numerous to list. It is perhaps worth mentioning that most were light fawn in colour. One of the best-known stud dogs was Toby of Studbergh.

Clunie of Kelwall (UK import), foundation bitch of the Shayla kennels in Canada.

Lyn and Walter Pratt of the Kelwall affix have been in the breed for many years. I first knew them around 1960. Their basic stock was Buttonoak and I well remember their two bitches, Bess and Tess, both deep red. The Kelwall kennel remained small, but nevertheless successful: Darrel, Derry and Frederick all became champions, the original Buttonoak breeding easy to see in all of them. Many will remember the Pratts for the hard work they put in to establish the brindle. They are still in the breed today but, alas, not very active.

Jim and Ethel Leeson established their Pitman's kennel in the 1960s. They were no strangers to dogs, as they had also bred Bull Terriers, and they quickly rose to the top with Ch Pitman's Gentleman Jim, winner of

Ch Sharwell Mean Mr Mustard of Pitman.

several CCs. All the subsequent male Pitman's can be traced straight back to him. He was also BIS at our Golden Jubilee Show. Type, size and movement have always been the priority of the Pitman's kennel, which has produced several champions at home and abroad. Probably their best-known dog was Ch Sharwell Mean Mr Mustard, top winning show dog and top stud for around six years. Mustard sired many CC winners and his influence will be felt in the breed for many years, particularly his remarkable temperament which he passed on to his progeny and their offspring. It may not be general knowledge that this dog was within an hour or so of being put down when Jim took him over. I do not consider him the best ever from this kennel (as a show dog, that is) but I am sure he will long be remembered in Bullmastiff history, probably as one of the best of recent years.

Jim Leeson is also one of the most successful breeders of brindles. His Pitman's line will continue to influence the breed's development for many years to come.

Dorothy M Price's Lombardy kennel came into Bullmastiffs in 1950 with a bitch, Braid of Bulmas, sired by Ch Branch of Bulmas. Unfortunately she never had a litter. On her death another bitch was acquired within four or five days. This is the only time a Bullmastiff has not been at Lombardy in all these years. Defiant of Lombardy, a Buttonoak-bred bitch, was the foundation of the line. Mated to Favian of Tipdixon she produced Marci, an exceedingly dark red. Marci sired Ch Harvester of Lombardy (page 27), who quickly brought the kennel to the top. Lombardy is probably one of the only true line-bred kennels, as both the male and female side of the pedigree were direct Ambassador of Buttonoak breeding. Unfortunately the line diversified in recent years but is still traceable back to Defiant. The same principle of close breeding still applies today. Successful Lombardy breeding is behind many overseas kennels.

Mr and Mrs Harris of the Bunsoro affix started in Bullmastiffs around 1970 with a bitch, U-Bonny Blonde. This bitch, when mated to a Naukeen dog of considerable size, produced their first champion, the well known Ch Bunsoro Cloudburst, himself a top-sized dog. This was the beginning of the Bunsoro line, which has had considerable success over the last 20 years, making up several champions cast in the same mould as Cloudburst (see page 27). The Harrises have established a line based on their own beginnings but incorporating several other lines. The reason they have remained at the top over all these years is probably because they have kept to their original idea that size is of great importance to the breed. Brindles have also been a feature of this kennel in the last few years, many getting to the top.

Tom and Dorothy Massey of the Todomas affix first came into breeding and exhibiting in the 1970s, although they had owned Bullmastiffs for many years. Basing their line on Mr and Mrs Harris's Bunsoros, they quickly rose to the top, producing several notable champions. Later, going out to Jim Leeson's Pitman's, they have established a clear line of their own. They too have had considerable success with brindles.

Ch Bunsoro Cloudburst.

Naukeen Bullmastiffs, belonging to Granville and Doreen Blount, is one of the longest established kennels in this country at 35 to 40 years old. Their line, built up from various sources, has had considerable success world-wide. Many champions have been made up by following a policy of keeping within the Naukeen line. Other breeders have had spectacular successes by using dogs from this kennel. Still going strong today, the Naukeen kennel still has much to give to our breed.

The Graecia kennel of Alan and Mavis Rostron is one of the better-known kennels today. I have known the Rostrons since the early 1960s. I believe they started with a quality bitch from Edna Goodhall. I recall them mating her to Ch Harvester of Lombardy to produce a top class red dog, Graecia Hotspur. Sadly, his early death prevented this dog from reaching his full potential; to me he was perhaps the best ever from this particular kennel. For some years the Rostrons did not seem

Ch Harvester of Lombardy. Photograph courtesy of Mr H Price.

Ch Graecia Centaur, official mascot of Q Mess, HMS Manchester.

to hit the high spots, but they were building a line. Their first great success came with Ch Graecia Centaur, an outstanding fawn dog who was awarded BOB at Crufts. Since then they have had a run of champions, all cast in the world mould.

There are several other notable breeders, but I think these are the main lines that have carried on a systematic breeding programme. All have common ancestry but this will be so far back in the pedigrees that it has very little effect on today's Bullmastiffs; with each generation the great sires fade farther into the background, losing their influence.

This is how I see the breed over the years I have been interested in it. Others may perhaps see it differently. I think it is fair to say that this last 50 years has seen the emergence of the Bullmastiff we have today. Many breeders have contributed something to this development. The breed made steady progress up until our Golden Jubilee Show in 1975 – probably the finest show of Bullmastiffs ever seen, and I doubt if we shall ever see such quality again. Since then there has been a great expansion in numbers in the breed, bringing with it an inevitable deterioration in overall quality. The good ones are still there to be seen but, regrettably, too many pet quality Bullmastiffs appear in the show ring and, even worse, are being bred from. I feel that the breed as a whole should take stock of itself and decide just where it is going. To lose what we dedicated breeders and exhibitors have achieved would be a disaster.

We have developed a Bullmastiff far different from that of our ancestors. Today our best have good square skulls. Muzzles are short, perhaps too short for my liking; I prefer them one third of the overall head length. Mouths are particularly good, with perfect or near-perfect level bites, the broad underjaw with teeth in a straight line giving a square-cut appearance to the muzzle. Though it is often said heads are not everything it is a hard fact that without a good head the Bullmastiff is nothing!

I also feel that there is too much variety of type and size and that more attention should be paid to what the Breed Standard actually says. There is little doubt that one area we could improve is the hindquarters. Far too many lack muscle power and are straight (perhaps a better description would be 'upright') in stifle. Many breeders seem unable to understand what good back ends are. There is a good old saying, 'If it's built right it moves right.' How true that is!

Ch Pitman's Gentleman Jim, BIS Golden Jubilee Show.
Photo: Mr H Price.

The Brindle Bullmastiff in Great Britain

It is probably entirely due to Mr and Mrs Warren (not to be confused with our present-day Gerald Warren) of the Harbex kennel that brindles did not become extinct during the second world war. They alone managed to bring this colour through these difficult years, and to them must go all of the credit for providing the base on which to build this colour. If they had not done so the colour would have had to be reintroduced from another breed. Certainly, in the early post-war years Ted and Florrie Warren were the only ones interested in breeding this colour. In view of the popularity of the brindle today I find this strange. Their most notable brindles were Grim and Chips of Harbex and it is a fact that every brindle in Great Britain today is descended from Harbex stock.

The brindle remained almost unnoticed until in the early 1960s two entirely separate kennels took up the

Lombardy Raffles, Best Puppy Golden Jubilee Show.
Photo: Mr H Price.

Canadian Champion Brutus of Ellisdene.

Brindles are now of high quality and hold their own
with reds and fawns.

colour almost simultaneously. The late Mrs L Parkes of the Silverfarm affix bought a brindle dog, Sealskin of Harbex, not a very good specimen of the breed. Walter and Lyn Pratt of Kelwall took one of their red bitches to a Harbex dog to be mated, and this was the foundation of both kennels of brindle Bullmastiffs. Both soon made probably the greatest step forward for this colour: Walter and Lyn produced a good red brindle bitch and Mrs Parkes bred the famous Copper of Silverfarm. Both were shown fearlessly, yet neither got the success they deserved, as many judges were reluctant even to consider a brindle.

Mrs Parkes continued to breed and exhibit the colour against all odds, often standing unnoticed in the class. She was a lady of great determination; a lesser person would have given up the struggle.

It is perhaps of interest that her breeding policy was to mate her brindle bitches to Mrs D M Price's red dogs to keep the correct colour (dark or black markings on a red or orange background).

Walter and Lyn Pratt were still concentrating on the brindle and bred the first brindle champion for many years, Ch Bonnie of Kelwall. He was one of my favourites, though not perhaps everyone's choice; he was well exhibited and won several CCs in his career. He also proved a stud dog, siring good brindles. It is worth mentioning that 'Clyde' was the result of a brindle/red mating.

By now the brindle was gaining in popularity and several prominent kennels were interested. Harry Collias (Oldwell) bred and exhibited several very good dogs, while Ralph and Ruth Short (Bulstaff), Douglas Oliff and Granville Blount (Naukeen) were also active. Mrs D M Price (Lombardy) had some success following a mating to Ch Clyde. Probably one of the most prominent brindle enthusiasts is Jim Leeson (Pitman's). His Ch Pitman's Deputy, a most prolific sire, will be found in many pedigrees. Pitman's Smart Alex, another prominent sire and in my personal opinion the best brindle ever, Pitman's Ambassador and Ch Pitman's Dark Prince have sired many of today's brindles.

It is fair to say that the brindle today is the equal of any self colour, in many cases the superior. It has had a difficult time, but the hard work put in by these dedicated people has now paid off.

CHAPTER THREE

How to choose a Puppy

Chizelhurst Chief of Rianel.

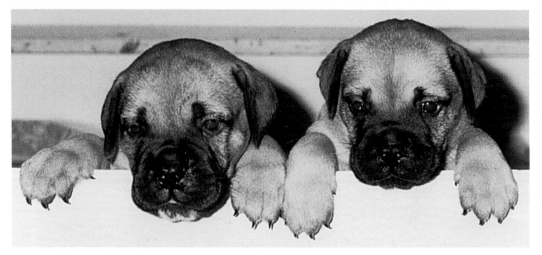

D & L Mylek's Wildwinds Cherokee Warrior and Wildwinds Casa Mice.

In the garden: Heroguardian Lady Ana Solo (Sadie) aged 19 months, with Anna Perry aged 13 months.

What Makes a Puppy Special?

Why is every puppy so cute? Like everything else in life, beauty is in the eye of the beholder. What most people do not realise is that their concept of beauty has evolved as a result of incidents that have occurred throughout their lives. Was it the way your parents did certain things? Was it a memory left behind after some pleasant occasion in your life? Whatever it was, each person has individual tastes and it is the gratification of these that brings happiness.

The reasons are just the same when it comes to a Bullmastiff puppy. Ask yourself why you'd like a Bullmastiff. What made you first decide to take a puppy home to be part of your life? The chances are somewhere, sometime you saw a Bullmastiff that just stole your heart and now you want to fill that memory by taking one home to be a part of your life.

Visiting the Breeder

What do you look for when you visit a breeder to choose your puppy? To the layman most puppies look the same no matter what breed, so make sure that you do not make a hurried choice and take the wrong puppy home.

If you want a nice, loving, good old-fashioned pet to take for walks, someone to keep you company at night, someone to love, with never a thought of showing or breeding, you do not need to read any further. Let your heart decide, go to the end of this chapter and start reading again at **Ready to Go**.

If you are looking for a show dog, your choice will have to be more selective. Most breeders will let you see the litter at about eight weeks of age, a very special age to which most people do not really give enough importance.

Try to see mother and pup together. Hopefully, Ch Rianel Gilda of Chizelhurst's puppy will inherit her temperament.

Between the time of birth and four weeks of age, puppies investigate anything new. This is nature's way of making sure that newborns familiarise themselves with their territory for security's sake. When danger threatens, the pups will run to the mother or the den for safety, ensuring survival.

Between the age of four and eight weeks, the puppies will reverse this attitude. Instead of running to everything new, they run away and reject anything different. This is another of nature's survival tactics. In the wild the mother usually takes her pups out of the den after four weeks and introduces them to the world. At this stage pups stay close to her, or to the den when she leaves to go hunting. At the sign of anything new and strange, instead of running to investigate as they would have done a week before, the pups run to the things they know to be safe: the den and the mother. This ensures survival, preventing them from being eaten as a result of running towards a predator.

What does this mean to you as a prospective puppy owner? In the first weeks of adoption, your puppy will be very anxious and nervous of new situations. As a new owner you must be patient and reassure the little dog if he baulks or reacts to anything new in a scared or nervous fashion. If you do this you will replace the

This litter has been reared in the warmth and comfort of an indoor home.

Motherhood is tiring!

Clean and content puppies.

Bullmastiff bitch cleaning her sleepy puppy. Pup's eyes are not yet open.

mother in the puppy's mind and develop a bond between you and the little dog, ensuring a well-adjusted pet that will not jump or over-react at the slightest thing.

When you go to see the breeder and the new litter, ask the breeder to let you see the parents. If both are not available there will usually be a photo of the father at least, and the mother will be there with the puppies. Remember that the puppy will grow up to resemble one or both of the parents to some extent, so take a careful look at the mother and father. If you do not particularly like what you see, leave immediately. If you stay, the puppy will win your heart anyway and you will end up with a dog whose appearance you do not like. According to the Bullmastiff standard, all Bullmastiffs should look the same, but this is never true in life no

Tracey Baby of Gamekeeper. Photo: R A Follentine.

matter what you consider. There will be minor differences in looks, colour and type. So if you do not like the parents, go home. There will always be another day for you to choose a puppy. You will have the love of this dog for many years, so do not choose in haste and repent at leisure.

So you have decided you like the look of the parents, that is why you are still here. Good. Now we must get down to the serious business of how to choose. Bear in mind that each line of dogs has a particular growth pattern, and only the breeder can tell you what it is; all the following advice will be modified by this fact. However, it will give you some pointers as to which questions to ask, and certain things are true no matter what the growth patterns are.

Early socialisation.

Puppy Parts

We will start by taking the individual parts of the dog, and go over them one by one.

The head

Even at the tender age of a few weeks, the head (cranium) of the Bullmastiff will be in evidence as a cube: whichever way you look at the head it will be square. This viewing does not include the muzzle, jaw or ears; just the head itself. You should be able to see a square head easily.

Looking at the head from the top or the front, the eyes should be at the front corners of the head. Eyes closer together indicate a narrow head or incorrect positioning of the eyes which will give an unnatural appearance. The attachment of the ears should be in line with the positioning of the eyes, so that the eyes are at the 'front' corners, and the ear attachment at the 'back' corners.

This will ensure you have a dog with a wide-set, square-looking head. At this time in the puppy's life

Upper Crust Bullmastiff puppies, approximately eight weeks old – ready to go to their new homes.

the ears will look exceptionally big and may hang down to the bottom of its jaw. The only guide to the adult animal is the parents.

The muzzle
The vertical attachment of the muzzle should be below the eyes and the width of the muzzle at this age should appear almost as wide at the front as it does at the point of attachment. In profile, the puppy may appear to have a large lump on the bridge of its nose. This is perfectly normal. This 'extra' nose will be displaced in the next few weeks as the puppy's muzzle grows. When you check the teeth, the bite should be level, or slightly overshot. Overshot? Yes! The puppy's muzzle is made up of the upper mandible, which is attached to the skull, and the lower jaw, which grows independently from the mandible. The two parts see-saw as the puppy grows, so if the bite is as described the chances are your puppy will end up with a correct bite. If the teeth are undershot at this age, you stand a good chance of the mature dog having a bad underbite. The extent to which this occurs will depend on the line and you must ask your breeder about this. Inside the mouth, the incisor teeth should be even and the canines well spaced. The canines give the dog the wide, square muzzle so a puppy with narrow canines will result in a snipey-nosed dog.

The neck
The roly-poly puppy you see before you will one day be a big dog. Proportions will change as in every living animal. However, if you look at the parents and like the type of neck each has, and they are similar, the chances are the puppy's neck will be about the same. A puppy's neck is short anyway, but look carefully. If his head seems to be sitting in the shoulders, he may have little or no neck and even a puppy should be able to show a certain amount of neck at this age. If his head movement seems a little stilted, look elsewhere in the litter. Conversely, giraffe necks are equally as undesirable.

The body
Although only a diminutive of his parents, the squareness or otherwise of the body will be very

Chizelhurst Chimurenga at six weeks. Note the square proportions.

Chizelhurst pups (aged 6 weeks) learning to feed from individual bowls.

evident. Stand the puppy up on a level surface and you should see easily whether the dog looks long in the body or short in the leg. When viewed from the side, the distance from the fore chest to the back of the thighs should roughly equal the height of the dog at the top of the shoulders (withers) even at this age. You will also be able to see if the puppy has sufficient brisket which should reach at least to his elbows. Take a look at the distance from the point of his elbow to the ground. Is it about half the height of the dog from the shoulder to the ground? Is his hock about one third of the height of the dog at the shoulder? Look at him from the front to make sure he is nice and broad

Four weeks old (bred by the author).

Five weeks old.

Seven weeks old.

Eight weeks old.

Three months old.

Eleven months old. Head change is most significant over the year's growth.

Chizelhurst Chanda aged 11 months.

in the chest; you do not want a narrow chested dog! His rear end should be almost as broad as his front. If it is considerably narrower than his front, you are witnessing Bulldog genes at work and your dog will grow up to be 'bully'.

Although these glimpses will be brief, and with full knowledge that he has a whole lifetime of growing ahead of him, such obvious glaring faults will be seen if they are extreme. Although it may fall within the widest interpretation of the standard, if the puppy is extreme in any area now the chances of changing dramatically are slight.

The tail

Many people look at puppies and try to guess their eventual size by the enormity of its paws. You are looking at the wrong place, however; all that you will be able to tell is that a Bullmastiff has enormous feet compared to a Border Terrier puppy! Allowing for the absence of crank or stunted versions, take a look at his tail. In the mature Bullmastiff, the best kind of tail should reach the hock. What about the puppy you are considering? Go on, take it and see where it reaches. A puppy whose tail reaches to or past his hock is probably a big dog in the making. The reverse also applies.

A Last Check

Before you snatch the puppy up and run home, a few more tips. Put him on the floor and watch him run around. The movement should be easy, balanced, and not narrow or single tracking. No glaring structural faults like cow hocks. This would show faulty skeletal structure.

What about his colour? In most cases, Bullmastiffs do not turn out to be the colour you expect when they are puppies. At birth most puppies are very dark, sometimes appearing black. The darker the puppy at birth the richer and deeper the colour at maturity. The dark colouring gradually goes until at about one year the colour is true and clear. The last vestiges of this darkness are usually a line down the back and the tip of the tail. So this is quite normal, unless the parents are still covered with a sooty shading, called pencilling, in areas such as the chest, neck and face. The standard is very specific that the colour has to be clear. If your puppy's parents are like this, your puppy will probably be the same. This sootiness is produced by too close a breeding, or by failing to adhere to the correct colour breeding patterns as first described by Eric Makins and Arthur Craven, two Bullmastiff pioneers from the early part of this century. This comment refers to fawns and reds, not brindles.

The standard permits a small amount of white on the chest. The white is referred to as permissible but undesirable, except for a small white patch. The operative word here is small: it does not mean white blazes reaching from the chin to the navel. Such dogs still appear in the show ring and, while judges endorse their presence with awards, such deviations will perpetuate. The presence of any white indicates the presence of Bulldog genes, of which the Bullmastiff carries 40%. If your puppy shows more white than an area about the size of a 50 pence piece, talk to the breeder. Some lines that show a little white at a few weeks lose it as the chest of the dog develops and in some cases seems to 'fold inwards'. Although this does not alter the genetic involvement, visually it reduces and sometimes disappears altogether.

Ready to Go

So you have gone through all the above and you have not left yet. Well, I suppose all that matters now is to pick the right one and be on your way. Right? Wrong! Talk to the breeder about the type of dog you would like to fit in with your family structure. Do you want a quiet dog, a barker, a dominant one, or a quiet pet to take with you wherever you go? The only person who can point out these things is the breeder. He knows his dogs, his line, his puppies' dispositions and whom they will suit best. Discuss these points truthfully and candidly because the one thing that you, the breeder, and the puppy do not want is your returning in a few days time, puppy under your arm, with a distressed look on all your faces telling everyone that you are not compatible. Be sensible: talk to the breeder.

If you are the tiniest bit hesitant, go home and come back tomorrow. The breeder will understand and appreciate your action. One thing for which you must strive is that you, the breeder and the puppy are totally happy about the step you are about to make.

Blewbore Dark Storm (Tojo) at 11 weeks socialising with five year oldRobert Perry.
Courtesy of A R Perry and H Clayton.

Baker St Struck By Lightning. Paw size at this age (12 weeks) does not necessarily indicate the likely size of the adult dog.

Going Home

If you can answer 'yes' to all the questions asked in the above section you will soon be the owner of a Bullmastiff puppy. A reputable breeder will advise you when the pup was wormed, the correct worming programme to follow and when he is due for his first vaccination. In the United Kingdom, the puppy is unlikely to have been vaccinated whilst still with the breeder unless you are purchasing an older puppy; in this case be sure to collect the vaccination card with the puppy.

One more thing before you go. Talk to the breeder about his feeding programme. He has raised the parent dogs you liked so much and a fine litter of puppies. This did not happen by accident; it was by careful planning, knowledge and expertise. Your breeder will be only too pleased to provide you with a puppy pack which will contain all the information you need to know in the first important year of your puppy's life. If at any time you need further advice or help, do not ask the man next door; ask your breeder, who will willingly help you.

Congratulations! You are now the proud owner of a fine Bullmastiff puppy.

Robert Perry, Tojo and friend.

Information Sheet
Below is a typical information sheet issued to each new owner by the **BUNSORO Kennels**.

DIET SHEET

Breakfast
2 egg yolks and half a pint of goat's milk, thickened with rice or semolina pudding.
Calcium and Canovel tables, <u>or</u>
2 poached eggs, 2 slices of toast, drink of goat's milk and honey, half tin sardines in oil.

Dinner
450g (1lb) meat with puppy meal (biscuits)
1 teaspoon of bone meal powder
1 drop of cod liver oil (I make hole in top of bottle), <u>but do not give in hot weather</u>.

Afternoon
Drink of goat's milk and honey.

Evening meal
Same as dinner <u>minus</u> cod liver oil.

REQUIREMENTS

Canovel or Vetzyme tablets

Calcium with Vitamin D tablets

Bone meal powder

Cod liver oil

Garlic and Fenugreek according to age

Honey

HINTS
A large marrow bone is useful to help puppy with new teeth (it keeps the pup from chewing your best chairs).
<u>Do not</u> let the puppy be picked up by the front legs.

<u>Do not</u> let children pick the puppy up – he will be too heavy and an accidental fall can damage young limbs and bones.

Bullmastiffs sometimes prefer to eat at night – so, if the puppy leaves the evening meal, take it up and put it down for the puppy when you go to bed (plus newspaper around the box).

Consult your vet for worm tablets – Second_____worming given_____/_____/_____

<u>Do not</u> let your puppy mix with other dogs or go outside your garden until after the **second** injection. It is wise to also have the Parvovirus injection, ask your vet about this.

<u>Do not</u> give egg white raw, only cooked.

A growing puppy requires plenty of rest.

CHAPTER FOUR

Maintenance and Grooming

Mutual admiration.

Nylabone products help to prevent tartar – and are fun to chew as well.

Did you ever wonder why some Bullmastiffs look stunning even to a bystander while others look quite ordinary?

Just as a clean, shiny car looks appealing compared to a dirty, unkempt one so it is with everything in life – including a Bullmastiff. The original Bullmastiffs were hard-working country dogs who spent most of their lives outside in the rain and inclement weather. Their one aim in life was to catch poachers, though later in the evening they thoroughly appreciated a warm place by the fire after a good supper. The gamekeepers kept their dogs healthy and strong but aesthetics were the last thing on their minds. As society changed, so more attention was given to the Bullmastiff's appearance as well as the work he did.

The Bullmastiff's weatherproof coat takes care of his insulation and waterproofing from the elements. However, modern-day owners expect their dogs to be compatible with their living conditions and to blend into the family structure without offence to the eye or nose, so some grooming is necessary. As has already been indicated, the Bullmastiff's coat type requires minimum work to keep it in good condition. However, there are a number of small maintenance items that will make your Bullmastiff look twice the dog.

The Head

Ears
The Bullmastiff's ears are drop ears and so hang down naturally. Their closeness to the side of the head can sometimes close off the opening of the ear canal, restricting air circulation, and the natural body heat causes the ear canals to overheat. This results in the ear canal filling up with a smelly, waxy substance that is very unpleasant and must be removed. Use a piece of cotton wool or a commercial cotton swab, but be sure to clean only the inside of the ear where you can see. Do not poke down into the ear canal, as any unqualified probing or a sudden movement by the dog can lead to a perforated ear drum. A mixture of mild soap and water or any patent ear cleaner will clean off this waxy substance. At the same time, look at the colour of the inside of the leather to see if it looks reddened or sore. If so, the chances are that the dog is carrying an infection. Do not attempt to remedy this yourself but contact your veterinary surgeon.

If a dark, smelly substance similar to wax still persists after the ears have been cleaned the dog may be carrying mites in the lower part of the ear canal. Once again, do not attempt to remedy this yourself. This is a job for a qualified vet, not an amateur.

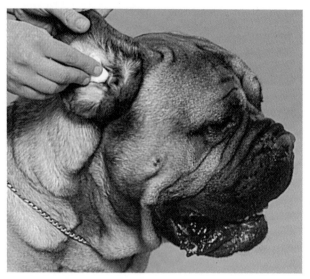

Cleaning the ears.

Eyes

The Bullmastiff does not have a haw eye like the Mastiff or St Bernard. Rather, he has a nice tight eye that usually remains trouble-free. This eye may need wiping from time to time to remove any air-borne detritus or 'sleep', but generally a Bullmastiff's eyes need little or no maintenance. Should you need to clean the eyes at any time, use a solution of boric acid. Commercial preparations are readily available at most pet stores. The Bullmastiff's eyes are clear and alert. If you notice ulceration or redness, it is possible he may have caught his eye on a stick or some sharp object. However, this may also be caused by entropion (see chapter 6). Whatever you feel the problem is, contact your vet.

Mouth

The Bullmastiff has a big, strong set of teeth. These should be kept clean at all times of tartar to reduce the chance of gum diseases and future loss of teeth at a young age. A good way of cleaning your dog's teeth and keeping his gums healthy is to give him an ample supply of hard dog biscuits to crunch on. It is a good idea to teach your puppy that frequent mouth inspections are a normal, every day procedure. This will permit checks for tartar which can be removed easily in the early stages with the edge of a sharp fingernail or a tooth scaler. I do not recommend that you give bones to your Bullmastiff, as his jaws are so strong that he is likely to gnaw fragments off the bone which will lodge in his stomach, causing problems.

Your local pet store will also supply a range of pet toys and chews that are specially formulated to clean the teeth whilst at the same time providing enjoyment for the dog. Nylabone produce a range of strong, durable chews that enhance the dog's dental care.

Whiskers

Whiskers may be removed if the owner prefers it, but any advantage is purely aesthetic. In some cultures the dog is seen always with all normal whiskers. If you wish to remove them for show or personal preference, certain safeguards have to be followed.

Although totally unlike human shaving, the initial sensation of removing whiskers will be strange to your dog. The safest way to remove them is to insert the

Inspect your dog's mouth and teeth regularly.

Keeping the teeth free of tartar.
Top left: a Nylabone Plaque Attacker Dental Floss. Top right: using a doggy toothbrush and toothpaste.
Bottom: Cleaning the teeth.

fingers of one hand under the lips of the dog's mouth and cut the whiskers off with scissors held in the other hand. Make sure the tips of the scissors point away from the dog's eyes in case he suddenly moves or objects to the procedure. Scissors with large, rounded tips can be purchased specifically for this task if the owner is a little nervous of having scissors around the dog's eyes. Some Bullmastiffs will allow their faces to be clipped with an electric clipper, but this takes co-operation, time, and a trusting dog.

The Legs

Feet

A Bullmastiff's feet should be strong, cat-like and well knuckled. This will not come about if he spends all his time lying or standing on a carpet in front of the fire, nor if he spends most of the time on concrete: this will splay his feet. The best medium for producing good feet is rounded, coarse gravel, about the size of pea gravel. This will make the muscles of his feet work hard, strengthening and developing them. If a dog run of this kind cannot be constructed, regular, brisk walks along gravel paths will produce the same results. Running in the wet sand on a beach will also be beneficial to the feet, as long as the salt is washed off after the run to avoid irritation or rashes.

Nails

The Bullmastiff is a large and heavy dog. To balance his frame he needs to stand upright with his muscles in perfect tone. He cannot do this if his nails are so long that he has to lean back on his pasterns. Continued posture like this will develop incorrect musculature in his pasterns and the balance of the whole dog will be affected. Sensible breeders will cut the nails short at a very early age to prevent the nerve, or quick as it is sometimes called, from growing too long. If this has been done it will be easy to cut the nails ever after without any worry of cutting them too short or causing them to bleed. The dog has no natural need to dig down burrows or underground so long nails are not necessary. When he is older, your Bullmastiff will thank you for looking after his feet.

Capping

Your Bullmastiff may not object to lying on hard surfaces (Bullmastiffs rarely do) but lying down heavily will eventually wear and tear the skin around his elbows and hocks. The skin gets knocked off and calloused and a hard cap of cartilage forms to protect the area. Hair grows very slowly on a Bullmastiff at the best of times, but once this happens, no more hair! The provision of a blanket or soft bedding will reduce or eliminate conditions that cause capping.

The Coat

The coat is waterproof and therefore usually looks good with very little attention. However, certain allowances have to be made if the dog lives outdoors in a dry, hot climate where the sebaceous glands of the skin have trouble keeping the coat oiled and shiny. Hot weather will also dry the skin and add to the problem. To keep the skin supple and well

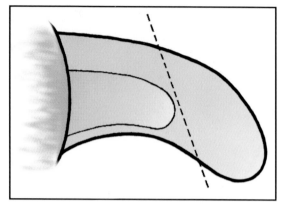

Trimming the nails. Illustration shows the position of the quick; be careful not to cut too close to it.

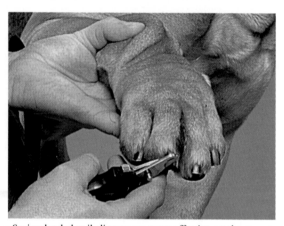

Spring loaded nail clippers are most effective on the strong nails of a Bullmastiff.

Regular exercise will help to keep the feet in shape.

oiled, a rubber hound glove should be used regularly with pressure all over the body to stimulate the flow of oil and massage the skin to a supple, healthy condition.

If the undercoat is causing the coat to be dull and harsh to the touch, it is time to remove it. A wire slicker brush will do a very fine job of this and the brush can be cleaned of its dead hair with a metal comb.

If your dog has been wormed recently he will shed the dead hair in his coat. This apparently short-haired dog will seem to produce an enormous amount of loose coat.

Something else that will cause a certain amount of confusion to your dog's coat is electric light. In the autumn the colder weather causes nature to prepare your dog for winter by increasing the quantity of his coat. This change is initiated by the reducing amount of daylight hours. If your Bullmastiff spends more and more time in your house as the weather cools off, the electric light will contradict his hormones' interpretation of the shortening days. The extra light on his coat will convince the hormones that the days are getting longer again and spring will seem to be arriving early. Conversely, the increasing light and temperatures of spring will cause him to shed his undercoat as his body temperature becomes too warm. The result is the shedding of the coat in readiness for warmer days of spring whether the time is real or not. This produces dog hair everywhere, a very frustrating experience for the house-proud owner. You have two alternatives: arrange warm, comfortable accommodation outside and leave nature to her own ways, or be prepared to use a slicker brush and comb daily to relieve your Bullmastiff of his excess coat and keep your furniture and clothing hair-free.

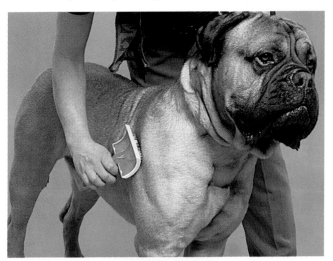

In many cases the remedy for a dirty coat is a good walk in the rain, or a drenching with a hose. Too many hot washes with shampoo will remove the oils necessary for a healthy coat, so hand washing should be done with utmost discretion.

Exposed extremities such as nose, lips, ears or even the spaces between the toes will benefit from an application of petroleum jelly or Vaseline. Your dog will appreciate such assistance to prevent cracking in hot climates. Remember not to do this

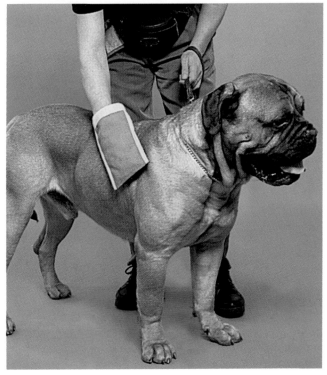

Using the slicker brush (top) and hound glove (below).

Use a small cloth to wipe away any drool.

to the pads; they act as a heat exchanger, so an application to this area will reduce heat loss and cause distress. If you do not believe it, watch for the damp footprints on your kitchen floor on a hot day.

Preparing for a Show

The Bullmastiff is a minimum maintenance dog. Besides the general grooming procedures described here, his natural appearance needs very little enhancing to get him ready for a show.

Depending on the cleanliness and coat condition, many Bullmastiffs go from the kennel to the show without the need for a bath. It will be necessary to clean your dog's coat if it has become soiled. Keep in mind that this working dog should have a waterproof coat; you do not want to turn up in the show ring with a Bullmastiff so recently bathed that his coat feels soft and fluffy.

You will need a few trial washes but usually, if you bathe your dog three to five days before a show, his natural oils will have returned. The required coat condition can be assisted by vigorous grooming with a rubber hound glove.

The only trimming prior to a show is the cowlicks down the back of the hind legs. These can sometimes become a little ragged and should be trimmed discreetly to enhance the line of the legs.

The flews of the Bullmastiff breed turn up at the back of the mouth, minimising any saliva or water loss in drooling or slobbering. Thankfully this removes the necessity for bibs, as seen on St Bernards, to protect the finished look while waiting to go into the ring. Some exhibitors carry a small cloth to wipe away any drooling caused through nerves, apprehension, or baiting.

Exercise

Your Bullmastiff is like a muscular athlete. When he first wakes up in the morning, some of his muscles may be stiff and tight. It is important to let your dog relax these muscles before starting exercise.

Even then, a Bullmastiff is not the kind of breed that wants to go on a five-mile jog. Exercise is necessary and important but it is amazing how little he needs to keep himself fit and healthy. Do not over-exercise your Bullmastiff, especially in the formative first year. If you take into account the weight your dog gains in that year it is easy to see that large amounts of cartilage are being formed at a very fast rate. If you over-exercise your dog, you will do a very good job of ruining his cartilaginous fibre and producing permanent damage to his skeletal structure.

A young Bullmastiff should be watched very closely. Once he has had enough exercise, let him rest. The exercise he has should be of his own making and not forced upon him by an over-enthusiastic owner who feels all big dogs need vigorous action. If you do this you will have an unhappy, and possibly permanently damaged, dog. At the age when everything is growing so fast it is easy for a young dog to over-rotate his hocks or any other joint, so treat him carefully. You should not think of him as a weakling, but as an adolescent in his formative years who needs guidance and wisdom. Depending on the growth pattern of your dog, half a mile a day may be all he wants to tackle. Some do more. The secret is to watch him. If he continuously sits down and is reluctant to follow, the chances are that he is tired and has had enough.

When he is about one year old formal exercise can begin. This should start off as good walks that do not tire him too much. Remember, it is the same distance there as back. Bullmastiffs do not mature physically until they are about three years old, so a little patience and understanding is required while this gentle giant is growing up. When he is able he will give you all the service you need and, provided you do not push him past his limits, he will reward your care with many years of faithful response.

The Older Bullmastiff

Depending on his lineage and the care he receives in the early part of his life, a Bullmastiff may start to become 'old' as early as six years of age. Each dog must be evaluated on its merits, but there are certain criteria to watch.

One of the earliest indications of pending old age is excessive amounts of stiffness and joint immobility. Arthritis can arrive very early in a Bullmastiff's life, and once arrived is there to stay. The tremendous weight on joints eventually takes its toll and, as the dog's regenerative mechanism slows down with his aging metabolism, the slide becomes one way. Luckily today's medications can relieve much of the distress as the dog moves further into his years, but always remember you will be treating a symptom and not the cause.

Your dog deserves the best care and attention.

When this time arrives for your dog, a positive aid to his situation is to ensure that he has a warm, dry place to sleep. A little padding on his sleeping area will help his sore joints, and you should make doubly sure that his sleeping quarters are draught-free. Keep trips outdoors in wet or cold weather to a minimum and be extra patient when he is trying to manoeuvre his large frame; it may be a very painful experience for him. Stairs and narrow halls may also be monumental challenges for him to overcome, so keep this thought in mind when considering quarters for your geriatric Bullmastiff.

The arthritis may also coincide with incontinence. At first this may only show as a mild odour on the bedding, but ultimately you must address the whole problem. Medications can help here, too.

The only other common problem as the dog advances in age is failing eyesight. This is often missed because he may hide this debility for some time by using his nose and knowledge of the house. When the problem is diagnosed, a kindness to your dog would be to leave items of furniture where they have always been, and return chairs to their usual places after use.

These are all symptoms of old age, and one or more of them will occur eventually. It is at that time in the dog's life that his owner has to think carefully about the future of the relationship with his canine friend. For those not used to coping with this, read **Eventide** in chapter 9.

CHAPTER FIVE

Housing

Crate for use as a doggy den in the house or car.

Inside or Out?

A major decision to be made by the senior members of the family is where your puppy is to sleep. At maturity a Bullmastiff does not take up as much room as you might first think, but it still presents a sizable space problem that must be considered ahead of time. When your new puppy arrives there will be many requests at night to take this little charmer to share one of the children's beds (or Mum and Dad's). Whoever is cited as the culprit, sooner or later a more definite decision has to be made as to where the new Bullmastiff puppy will sleep permanently. It is important for you to decide where this is to be early in the dog's life to avoid confusing him. Your Bullmastiff will want a place he can consider secure against cats and exuberant children, or just a place where he can sit quietly when life gets a little hectic.

Life will be strange to the new canine member of your family no matter what care is taken by the thoughtful owner. It is a good idea to settle the puppy into his routine as soon as possible. Like a young child, the little newcomer will quickly learn if one member of the family is willing to allow oversights when the other is not. For this reason, once you have decided whether to have inside or outside quarters, and assigned the sleeping quarters, you should keep to it regardless of the cries of woe and appeal that will arise in the first few nights from both puppy and humans. Develop your plan of strategy and remain firm. Your pup will then quickly realise there is no compromising and will settle down to the routine; house-training will soon be over and then you will have a nice, clean, happy puppy who is welcomed by everyone.

Inside

If you decide to keep the puppy inside the first challenge is house-training. When the puppy is put to bed after a riotous day of fun and play everyone is tired and of the same mind: sleep, no need to go outside. However, next morning when someone has to clean up after the little one, who will have been up longer than you, the mess and unpleasantness will be shared by all.

Puppies have an in-built aversion to soiling their own sleeping area. A good way to house train your puppy is to crate him at night, and choose a crate that is confining rather than a large one. The little puppy will hang on as long as he can as he does not want to lie in his mess. For your part, as soon as you are up in the morning, hurry him outside to your choice of toilet areas before he explodes. Bullmastiffs of all ages seem to produce a tremendous amount of waste matter: they must be hollow. This is your time to praise him generously, telling him what a good puppy he is, and do it with lots of gusto. It is much better than the alternative! Be prepared to take your puppy outside first thing in the morning, straight after each meal, and last thing at night. This amounts to at least six times each day. Up to the age of four months your puppy has very little muscle control over his inner organs so he needs to go outside every couple of hours and after each nap.

When your puppy has mastered this kindly act the next step is to allow him more liberty in his new indoor housing to see if he can be trusted until he goes outside. An enclosed area in the kitchen or utility room with a linoleum or tile floor is very forgiving in the case of accidents, and easy to clean up. Remember, control what you can. If he is good, expand the area and the trust; if he regresses, close back up. If you have to leave the house for a while, a large crate allows him freedom of movement but ensures no surprises await you on your return.

All this practice is a dry run for when he lives in the house all the time. When you are satisfied with the pup's house-training he will need a large basket or, as most people prefer, a large crate of his own. The large crate approach allows him his own in-house secure area and at awkward times, such as tradesmen coming and going, you can lock the door of the crate so you can be quite sure where he is. Crating him up saves the tradesmen a lot of worry!

The bedding area should be big enough to allow the Bullmastiff to stretch out, not just for luxury but for his health. A mature dog is likened to a muscular weight lifter. After spending many hours sleeping or resting the muscles sometimes become a little stiff or uncomfortable and it is necessary for your dog to stand, stretch and get the cramps out of them. Failure to do this will give your dog much discomfort. The breed is quite insensitive to pain especially when asleep so make sure his sleeping area has no sharp edges.

That a Bullmastiff is a large, heavy, muscled dog should be evident by now and, when he lies down, it is sometimes a great physical effort to do so quietly and gently. In many cases the dog will just drop down. After all, the shortest distance between two points is a straight line, and the Bullmastiff knows his physics! To save his joints, muscles, and general frame it is a good idea to provide him with enough padding in his bed to give him a little cushioning when he first lies down and while he sleeps. He will thank you in the morning. Your extra thought in providing such bedding also saves the capping of his joints described in chapter 4. When you do give him bedding be sure you treat it regularly for fleas, as such a soft, warm area is prime flea country.

Bullmastiffs need a considerable amount of water so, before he arrives at your house, decide whether to leave a dish of water with him all night or just through the day. The answer to this usually depends on your house-training successes, or lack of them.

You also need to consider how to position his bed. Strong as he is, he must not be housed where it is damp or draughty, or in a main thoroughfare. Put him in an out-of-the-way place, perhaps in a quiet corner or a dry, well-aired portion of your utility room; preferably away from the madding crowd, but in a spot from which he can investigate unknowns quickly without taking the laundry basket with him as he jumps up to see what the noise is about. He will always want to see what is going on but does not need to be in the main thoroughfare. You will appreciate a carefully chosen position when you are trying to cook supper or get the kids off to school, so think about all the options.

The bedding should be changed regularly to keep the doggy smell out of every household item and to check the flea situation. At certain times your Bullmastiff loses a lot of hair (see chapter 4). Regular bed changes ensure that dog hair is not mixed with every other household article in the near vicinity.

The picture shows a raised sleeping area to prevent draughts. In the background is a slide which can be lifted to allow the dog access to the outside run.

Outside

The Bullmastiff is well prepared for an outside life with his weatherproof coat, specially evolved for inclement weather. The original Bullmastiffs were used to living outside on their masters' estates, but modern day living puts more restrictions on the average owner than on the old-time gamekeepers. When a modern Bullmastiff is kept outside, consideration must be given not just to those factors considered in the Indoor section, but to every aspect of his life on his master's 'estate'.

The 'estate' must be clearly defined for the Bullmastiff. The safest way is to ensure that the exercise area and the whole back garden is fenced. In many cases the fence is not only to keep the dog in, establishing the limits of his territory, but to keep out casual guests such as children, meter readers, dustmen, postmen, unwanted dogs, and anyone else who should know better than to come into your back garden uninvited. The only safe way to do this is to enclose the garden with a fence at least 1.5m (5ft) in height, higher if possible. Bullmastiffs are not jumpers, but their weight can cause considerable damage. To offset this, a rail at about 1.5m high for the dog to jump against will prevent an unstrengthened fence from collapsing under the concentrated weight in one small area.

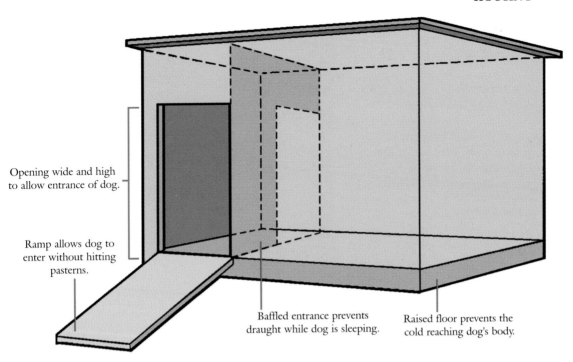

Opening wide and high
to allow entrance of dog.

Ramp allows dog to
enter without hitting
pasterns.

Baffled entrance prevents
draught while dog is sleeping.

Raised floor prevents the
cold reaching dog's body.

Plan of outside sleeping quarters for a Bullmastiff.

Wooden fencing is most suitable but, where this is not economically feasible, chain link is fine as long as the top is protected with a strengthened strand. Remember to make the 1.5m high rail, and do make the fence strong. It is amazing what a few jumps by a Bullmastiff can do to a fence. It is advisable to build your fencing so that the dog can see out. He will soon learn to ignore the less annoying problems if he can see what is going on outside.

The strength of a chain is as strong as its weakest link. This goes for the gate in your fence. It is a waste of time to secure your property with a safe fence only to have a gate swing open at a touch. Never forget that this area is your dog's territory, and he will not take happily to any stranger coming through the gate. Lock it, put up warnings (check locally for the correct wording) and, if necessary, install a bell. Remember, no matter how foolish the interloper may be, you and the whole of the breed fancy will suffer if you are negligent and someone gets hurt.

So now you have his environment safe and secure, what about his sleeping quarters?

If your garden is not particularly big it may serve as the whole dog run. In this case you need only provide the sleeping quarters. If, however, you have more land you may choose to build a dog run within the area to confine your dog when you are out or when you have guests.

In the latter case, pre-stretched panels of fence wire, chain link or other suitable fencing material can easily serve as a run for your dog. Ideally the run should be a minimum of 4m x 1m (12ft x 4ft), sloping, and allowing your dog easy access to water and food when necessary. If he is not going to be in the run for long, a gravel base will keep his muscles in fine trim, and the gravel can be raked level after use. Hygiene is the main consideration here. If your dog stays in the run long enough to produce quantities of faeces, a malodorous environment may result even if pick-up is regular, and gravel is not the best medium. In such cases, a concrete base with a slope of a minimum of 3.5cm per metre (0.5in per lateral foot) is advisable, with a drain on the lower end that takes the waste far away. Such runs are easy to wash and maintain in a hygienic state. One warning here though: long spells on a concrete run will cause your dog's feet to splay, so make sure there is plenty of time for him to relax on grass or on a gravel area to tone up his muscles.

All the indoor considerations apply when considering an outdoor sleeping area. There is also need for a weatherproof covering. The structure should be strong and large enough for the dog to stand up and walk around. He may find it awkward to settle if his muscles are aching and his movements are restricted and will therefore spend a very uncomfortable night trying to relax. The external opening should face away from the prevailing winds with a weatherproof flap to break the wind. Most Bullmastiffs eat the flaps sooner or later so it is best to work around this aspect.

Failing this an interior solid panel to deflect any incoming wind will help deter draughts. Draughts and damp are the main concerns. Most Bullmastiffs can put up with cold or heat, but dampness and draughtiness can contribute to the early onset of arthritis. An electric light bulb underneath the floor can sometimes be of value to ward off any such problems. It is not necessary to provide heated quarters but it is kind to keep the damp away. The kennel must be elevated from the ground to minimise dampness and thus decrease the incidence of the

ailments that affect dogs when they are allowed to lie on the damp ground.

The approach to the entrance of the kennel should be sloped rather than stepped. Some Bullmastiffs refuse to pick up their feet properly when stepping into their kennel and repeatedly bump their pastern joints on the step. In time this produces an ossial contusion, or bruising of the bone, which shows as a rather ugly, calcified lump on the pastern joint. This is not a pretty sight and will most certainly be disadvantageous to your dog in any show ring.

Outdoor bedding can take the form of straw or hay. Either will keep him warm at night and keep his coat clean and shining. It should be cleaned out weekly to prevent flea infestation.

Do not leave excess food outside as this will attract flies. Provide water in a bucket, or you can buy a mechanism that fits the garden tap and releases water only when licked. Placing both food and water utensils at chest height allows your dog to eat standing up and stretches his muscles in the right direction. To bend the neck right down and eat at the same time does not do much for digestion or the dog's neck muscles. Reaching up to eat will help him to develop strong pastern muscles and good neck musculature.

You now have the right environment, the right house, the right bedding and the right eating methods. By the time you have read this far you know all the ways to enjoy the company of your Bullmastiff.

Make the most of him while he is a puppy; he will soon be grown up. Watch him grow and learn together how to coexist in a way that is right for both of you and for everyone else around him. When he grows up perhaps you will think of breeding, showing or both. Well, you have gone much further than you thought you would at one stage, so why not look a little further still? The next steps are no more frightening or confusing than the ones you have just taken. Remember when you thought that was a big step? By this time you are a fully-fledged Bullmastiff fancier. So read on!

Large outside kennels with several runs for keeping more than one dog.

Outside housing with attached run, ideal for one dog or a mother with pups.

CHAPTER SIX

Training

Manwork.

Why, you may ask, does there have to be a section on training so soon after selecting your puppy? Everyone knows that sooner or later a dog has to be trained. Why not wait until later?

The cute little Bullmastiff puppy you just brought home is more than likely the whole centre of attention at the moment. Well, I cannot stress too many times that this little bundle of fun, probably about 9kg (20lb) at present, is going to be gaining weight at about 4.5kg (10lb) a month for the first year. At the tender age of nine months he will weigh about 40kg (90lb); and at one year will be well over 45kg (100lb). Time will pass quickly and you should understand one thing clearly: if at the age of one year you cannot control this large dog with commands to which he will respond, the chances are you will not be able to do it physically. This puppy will be stronger at one year of age than most of your family. Do not wait until then to find you have made a big mistake. No one likes a badly behaved dog, especially when he is bigger than everything else around him.

Start training your puppy as soon as he arrives home. This does not mean you have to take him outside immediately for formal obedience training. More realistically, his initial training will take the form of correction of his responses to new experiences, which will give the puppy paws-on experience.

Some owners feel that a big dog breed such as this demands a rough, 'manly' approach. If this means shouting loudly, intimidation, and physical coercion you are in the wrong breed. When fully grown, a Bullmastiff is a large, strong, well-adjusted dog. Do not forget that he was originally bred to overcome someone whose sole intent was to escape him by abusing him physically. A desperate man on the run does not care how he escapes; the only criterion is that he does. Shouting, swearing, kicking, screaming and physical violence were all part of a day's work in the Bullmastiff's routine job of catching poachers. Such abusive attitudes towards this dog in training will cause the dog to 'switch off' and become introvert; this is inherent in his genes. He will respond in no way at all to such treatment from you, grouping you mentally with the poachers. As a breed Bullmastiffs need firmness in training and repetitive consistency but, if you use only physical intimidation as a method of training, you may well suffer the same fate as the poachers who tried such tactics.

If you want to earn the trust and respect of your dog you must also give him trust and respect. A softly spoken word will go much further than a frustrated shout. Bullmastiffs are cool, logical animals. Just when you think he is not taking any notice and is being rather slow on the uptake, he is working out the whys and wherefores and, when he has had time to think about it, he will surprise you next time out. A stern 'No!' from the one he loves and respects is all the correction he will need. Conversely, generous praise when he does right will motivate him to try harder.

Another thing to ponder when you start training is the attitude of the Bullmastiff breed in general. Someone once compared a Bullmastiff in training to a piece of wet string: if you are careful you can lead it anywhere, but at no time can you push it.

One last comment before discussing different forms of training: the Bullmastiff, as described in chapter 2, has been used through the ages as a guard dog. No amount of ignoring this fact by bribing him with treats or using any form of discipline will remove this temperament. To do so would be to create a new breed that physically resembled the Bullmastiff but was nothing more underneath than a dummy. Remember when you are training the family pet that, underneath the exterior of the hospitable, loving pet you know as your own, he is still a guard dog. Do not relinquish responsibility and become careless as you proceed through life. You know his limitations, temperament, and breed history. The dog owner coming towards you in the park with a yappy, snappy little dog (which, by the way, just wants to say 'Hello'), will never forgive you or the breed if something terrible happens to her dog.

Using the above as a framework, let us start the serious business of formal training. Training as a whole can fall under three broad categories: Obedience, Show, and Guard. The comments on each of these categories are not meant as substitutes for training manuals but as a guide to the new owner. For in-depth, comprehensive training you may have to contact a professional in your area, describe what you want to do, and proceed from there.

Obedience

Everyone admires a well-behaved dog no matter what breed it is. Conversely, a badly-behaved dog is shunned like an ill-mannered child. An understanding of how a Bullmastiff thinks and reasons will assist you in training your dog for obedience. The object of this advice is not to replace or modify any obedience instruction you may use, whether it is a book instruction or attendance at a group training session. The following is intended to help you show your new puppy what you require in the shortest

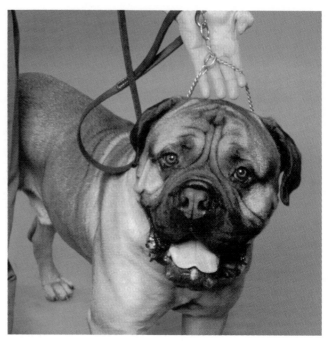

The correct way to put on a choke chain.

time and with the least resistance. He will become a very heavy subject should his attitude to obedience training be one of stubbornness or rejection.

Walking to heel

The Bullmastiff does not march along at a military step. Many Bullmastiffs seem to waddle or roll as they walk at a normal pace, the amount of waddle or roll depending on the amount of angulation in the rear quarters: the more angulation, the more roll. If you look closely you will see that this roll comes not from the hips, as first imagined by many people concerned about hip dysplasia, but from the sacroiliac area (the point where the spine joins the pelvis). Many Bullmastiffs provide quite a challenge in 'heeling', as their horizontal movement and wide chest present a sloppy heeling position when the handler attempts to position the dog's shoulder level with his thigh.

Training should start as soon and as young as possible (about four months), when the dog's attention is on everything except you. What you must do is make sure he is always watching you. To do this he must be in a position where his shoulder is level or slightly behind your thigh so that he can walk beside you and watch you at the same time. To do this use a 2m (6ft) training leash and a chain choke collar with the choker high up on the dog's neck close to his jaw, not down around his shoulders where there is no leverage. When the choker is in position there should be approximately 5cm (2in) of chain spare. Slipping the handle of the leash over your thumb (not your wrist: if he takes off after a cat you go with him, but with the thumb method you can let go quickly), position the dog at your left side with the leash taut across your thighs. Hold the excess of the leash in the right hand. Remember, the choker is high up on his neck so that, as soon as you command 'Heel!' and move off, your thighs project his head and the rest of him forward. You must have the choker high or he can baulk when you move off and hold you back, causing you to lose control. This sudden movement will cause him a little concern at first when he is moved in a direction he may not wish to go.

Once you are on the move his attention should be on you at all times. As soon as his attention is distracted, drop the excess of the leash you have been holding in your right hand and run (yes, run!) in the opposite direction (back the way you just came). The startling effect you will have on your Bullmastiff is obvious. After doing this a couple of times you can be sure he will keep his eye on you very carefully. After a few sessions your Bullmastiff will be heeling well, and not towing you down the road. Because of the leverage involved in the 'about turn' any person can do this, large or small. The main points to remember are the high choker, for leverage, and the use of the leash. As you move forward remember the command, loud and distinctive. Always use the same tone of voice and remember that, except for the call to 'come', these words are commands. Say them in that manner; they are not requests to your trainee to involve himself in a democratic discussion about behaviour.

The Sit
When you come to a halt during heelwork your Bullmastiff may or may not sit, or look around, or even wander off. Remember: control is the name of the game and you are supposed to be in control. As soon as you halt, be ready to move him into a sit. As he stops (and the choker collar is still high on his neck), pull up with the choker, push down on his rear and clearly command 'Sit!' The mechanics of this movement will nearly always result in a sit – sometimes not a pretty sit, but a sit. Some Bullmastiffs find it hard to lower their cumbersome rear to the ground at the same time as sitting close and tightly alongside the handler. At the finish of a good sit he should be square to you and his chest level with the front of your thighs. If the sit is not a good one repeat the heel procedure and as he goes to sit guide him into a good one. Until he gets the idea of what training is all about he may consider the commands as a harsh correction. Because of this it is very important to praise him highly when he does well to reinforce the positive things he has done. Always remember: for every negative be sure to manipulate a positive in there. I would not recommend using biscuits as a reward. The reason? What happens in an emergency situation when you have no reward? What do you think his reaction will be? Once again you are manoeuvring a large, bulky dog around and you must use your knowledge in the beginning to lever this unwieldy weight to your advantage.

The Recall
This is the only command that requests rather than orders the dog to do as he is bid. The reason is one of effect. If you call your dog to come in a voice like thunder, do you expect him to react willingly? The word must be inviting and attractive. Sometimes, if the Bullmastiff is in a comfortable sitting position, it is a little too much trouble for him to move his bulk to come to you. If this is the case, attach his leash, and as you call him to come give a hefty pull on the leash in your direction. You will soon convince him that, as you speak, a magical force propels him to you. The bewilderment sometimes is very evident on the dog's face and, like a superstitious person who thinks he has seen a ghost, he will move more quickly the next time. When he does, lavish praise on him, and he will be more than willing to respond when you try it again.

The Stay
The preceding examples show clearly that to control your Bullmastiff physically as a puppy in training you must anticipate the manoeuvrings of his large body. By thinking ahead and being ready you can easily complete the exercise without undue physical activity and convince your Bullmastiff you are in control at all times. You must never let a Bullmastiff know just how strong he is compared to you.

The easiest form of stay to teach is the 'Sit/Stay'. After you have brought your Bullmastiff to a satisfactory sit, using the palm of your right hand, bring it sharply across and in front of his face, as if you were going to slap him in the nose, and command 'Stay!'. You should then move a very short distance. Looking forward and using your peripheral vision, check to see if he starts to move and react before he has time to stand up. Back up and repeat the stay command. Once he is up you may have problems getting him to sit again. He will have lost the train of thought and your advantage will have disappeared. It is much easier to prevent this big dog from standing up and following you than to try and convince him to sit from a standing position against his will. When you have completed a successful exercise, return to the dog and finish on a positive note, praising him for his success.

The Down

From the sitting position it is a relatively easy procedure to get your Bullmastiff to lie down. The normal approach to this is to use the Bullmastiff's own weight to help you. Pull down hard and continuously on the leash towards the floor, simultaneously moving his front legs forward and giving the command 'Down!'. Most dogs will go down easily this way, but watch – if he is not comfortable as he goes down he may sit up again to reach a more comfortable position. If he does this you have lost the control, so hold the leash down tightly until he has settled himself properly in the down position.

Attitude

As you go through this training, always keep in mind that the Bullmastiff has a Mastiff mentality. Unlike Spitz type dogs (German Shepherds, Belgian Sheepdogs), who learn quickly, the Mastiff in your dog demands reason and logic. Quite often an exercise he could not do well today he may excel at tomorrow, once he has had time to think it out. You will never get blind obedience from a Bullmastiff where he will leap off a cliff or jump through a burning hoop; he is a dog of cold logic. As a result of this you may have to repeat a procedure more times than you think you should to convince him, but once he has it his retention is as good or better than that of most breeds.

His Mastiff mentality will also tell you when he has had enough. In many cases he will just lie down in disgust. This is time to quit as far as he is concerned. He will not be over-anxious to attend the next training session, either. Anticipate this reaction and finish the session on a positive rewarding note so that the next time you train he will remember it as a fun time, not a boring, unhappy time. It is better to have many small sessions than one long one. About 15 minutes each time is adequate. A final piece of advice: do not train after he has just eaten since a dog with a full stomach is not a willing pupil: sleep calls.

Showing

How do you feel about taking your dog into the ring and winning his championship? Most people shy away and quickly decline this invitation on grounds of inexperience and ignorance of proceedings. Well, now you will have no excuse. Read the following and be prepared to venture out into the spotlight.

Spotlight? No, not really. The first sensible thing to remember is the show is not for you; it is for your dog. Many novices work up a nervous condition while waiting outside the ring and are almost wrecks before the proceedings begin. Let me tell you as a judge, you are not the important part of the partnership entering the ring; your dog is. When your number is called the eyes of the judge and the public are watching what is at the end of the leash: the bottom end. Once you can register this through your trembling the fright will be gone. To be honest, after you have paid your entry fee and your travel costs to the show plus, perhaps, your overnight stay you have approximately two minutes in which to show the judge the mettle of your dog. If you are placed anywhere other than Best of Breed, or Best Puppy in Breed, your time is over until the next show.

The point to be made here is that in those two minutes you will be fully occupied showing off every part of your dog's conformation in an effort to convince the judge you have the best dog. In fact you will be working so hard you will not have time to reflect on whether your hair is a mess or you are handling correctly. In that two minutes you will be working with every ounce of energy on the dog and, if you are doing it well, all eyes will be on the dog, not you. Remember that!

I am sure you will have butterflies the first show; everyone does. Once you realise that you have paid for your time and you are going to get your money's worth, the time will be over: hopefully you have won, and it was not really all that bad, was it? The next show will be 10 times easier.

Always remember when you enter the show ring that it is a show, and the operative word is 'show'. You could have a superior dog to your competitor, but if you handle poorly and he does it well, who will come out with the ribbon?

The ring, actually a square, is approximately 12m x 12m (40ft x 40ft). This ring is the domain and kingdom of the judge. While you are in the ring, remember this and pay attention to the judge's and steward's instructions. The judge will always tell you what he wants and will ask you to do certain things for reasons of his own to pick the best dog. A brief visit to the ring before your breed is due to be shown will give you a good idea of the judge's method of operation and help you to avoid going in unaware of his ring procedure.

The steward will call you to the edge of the ring just before you are due to go in. It is your responsibility to be waiting at the entrance; the steward will not go looking for you. If you are not there you could be marked absent and lose your chance to show that day. Wait quietly until the steward calls your number and pay attention when he tells you where to go in the ring. Always remember: in the time you are in the ring you must do all you can to present the best of your dog to the judge. Never place yourself between the dog and the judge; make sure you manoeuvre yourself into a position on the opposing side of your dog to the judge. If he looks up and sees something about your dog that catches his eye it will leave a lasting impression.

A typical procedure will be for the judge to ask all the exhibitors to gait their dogs around the ring for him to see the relative movements. Following this usually is a detailed inspection of each dog, then an individual gaiting so each dog's movement can be studied. After completing this step the judge will make his selection of the best dog. Depending on the country in which the dog is shown the sequence of placement and awards will differ. The ultimate award is to determine the best example of the breed shown, in this case the best Bullmastiff. The best Bullmastiff will then be shown against other best dogs in the Working Group (Akitas, Malamutes and others). The best dog from this Group selection will be shown against the best dogs from the other groups (for example, best herding dog and best sporting dog). The final award is that of the Best in Show (BIS). Depending on the country of exhibition, the winning dog gains points at each level. These are collated over the year to determine the best dog at breed and group level and the dog's standing overall compared to all the other dogs shown in the country for that year.

This is a simplification of the whole procedure but serves to explain the general concept of conformation showing. For more information contact your local show Secretary or Kennel Club.

While in the ring you will be asked to complete certain procedures, and words may be used that you have not heard before. To assist you as a novice the following may be of help.

Gait
This refers to moving your dog. A Bullmastiff should be moved as fast as is necessary to show his best movement: not walking or galloping, not too fast, not too slow. Practice will tell you which is the best speed for your dog. Do not judge your gait speed by others around you. Your dog's best gaiting speed will depend on his conformation. Use a video, full length mirror or have an experienced friend watch you to guage the most appropriate speeed to show off your dog.

Before you attend your first championship point show it is a good idea to attend one of the many sanction or puppy matches arranged by local dog clubs. These practice shows are a good introduction for young puppies and novices alike to the world of showing. The atmosphere at these shows is much less competitive and those attending are more than willing to give tips and advice to the newcomer.

Stack

'Stack' is the term used when the dog is positioned in his best stance to show off his conformation. A Bullmastiff should stand 'four square'. This means all of his four legs support his body as if they were the legs of a table. The front legs should be vertical and placed beneath his shoulders so that he displays his broad chest well and supports his upper body fully. If you move his legs too far forward he will resemble a rocking horse, and will also throw his forequarter weight backwards instead of over his front legs, causing his back to dip. A strong, straight top line is important. His back feet should be placed in such a position as to give him a good, straight top line, and preferably vertical hocks. The positioning of his back feet will depend on the precise amount of angulation in his stifle (knee) and the length of his back. Too much angulation will often necessitate the back legs being placed so far back to give the correct top line that the dog will appear long backed.

The head should be held up in such a manner as to show off his expression, with ears forward and a good arch of neck. This last action can be enhanced by pulling up on the choker collar at the same time as pressing down on the withers area. Be sure the choker collar is positioned under his chin in a manner that does not collect up the extra skin and makes your dog look as if he has double chins.

Examination

The judge comes towards you to examine your dog. If you have done your practice correctly your dog should stand still. Younger dogs are excused a little fidgeting but older dogs are expected to allow examination without fuss. Remember, show your dog, not your arm or jacket or skirt. Keep yourself out of view of the judge no matter what it takes to do so.

The judge will normally ask to see the dog's teeth, or bite. At this point you are expected to open the dog's mouth to show the front teeth and their respective bite. Some judges will do this themselves but generally they will ask you. Some Bullmastiffs have a very thick pad of skin at the front of their bottom lip so flashing the teeth is not easy. As you show the teeth you must also maintain the dog in a stationary position, so be sure you have practised well before going in front of a judge. It is wise to carry a piece of cloth in a handy pocket so that when you have shown the teeth you can quickly and unobtrusively wipe away any saliva on the dog's face or your hands. When the judge has examined the head he will examine the rest of the dog and you will have to move away from the side of your dog for him to do this. To maintain control over your dog hold the head tightly. This will stop a nervous or inquisitive dog from turning his head to interfere with the judge's examination. At the same time you can control the balance of the dog by deftly manoeuvring the head to prejudice the weight positioning of the dog over his feet and keep him standing as he is. Practice will show you how to induce the dog to move parts of his body as you wish, using his head as a remote control device. This will keep the dog in a standing, stationary, show position for the judge's examination. Many judges take one last look before moving on to the next dog so do not relax too soon.

Moving your dog

This is when you will be asked to move the dog individually. This is your moment to shine, so listen carefully to what the judge asks you to do. You should have practised the following movements at home and you can also watch other exhibitors on the day to see what they do.

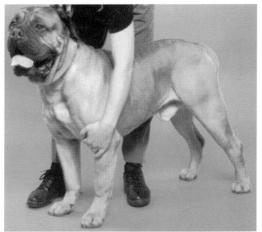

Stacking the dog for the judge. **Top left:** Set the left front leg first by grasping the elbow (never the foot). This is the first part of the dog that the judge will see, so position it first. **Top right:** Move the right front, again by the elbow. This allows the dog's weight to balance over the leg. **Centre left:** Holding the head up with a firm hand on the collar to prevent the dog moving out of the stack on the front, set the outside back leg by grasping the hock. If the judge were to look at your dog now, he is complete enough in the stack. **Centre right:** The final setting of the dog by adjusting the inside back hock. This can also be used to adjust the dog if he is leaning in the wrong direction or his topline is incorrect. **Bottom:** A beautifully stacked dog.

The Triangle

This is a common movement in which the dog is moved from the judge directly down the side of the ring. At the first corner he is moved to the next corner, at right angles to the initial movement. The dog is then turned to come directly back to the judge. In such a large breed as the Bullmastiff, it is accepted protocol to use your body as a pivot point to turn the dog at the second corner. Although this blocks the view of the dog momentarily, doing a full turn in insufficient space can look clumsy and detract from your dog's gait. When you approach the judge do not bowl him over with a runaway dog. As you near him, the

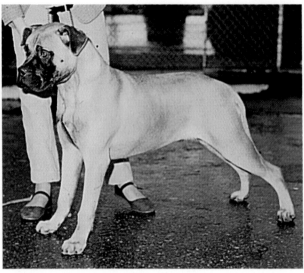

Poor stack; dog is overstretched and wide both in front and behind.

judge may signal for you to stop. This is your cue to stop your dog close to him in a superb show stance. This takes a little practice but it is very impressive if done nicely.

The 'L'

This movement is not liked by many handlers but is occasionally asked for by judges. The dog is moved as in the first two movements of the triangle but at the far corner, instead of moving directly to the judge, the steps are retraced. The trick in this is to teach your dog that at the about turn he will be coming back on the other side of you from that to which he has become accustomed. He will have to learn that he is expected to continue on this other side until he returns to the first corner, at which time he will pass in front of you onto his accustomed side to complete the remainder of the procedure. Although this is not asked for too many times you should practise it just in case. Remember: do not put yourself between the dog and the judge.

Using The Whole Ring

After the individual examination the judging is usually completed by the judge asking you to move your dog around the ring to the end of the line. At this time keep your eye on the judge, have your dog looking his best, and listen carefully for any instructions. If you are placed you will go into line by the position markers. If you are not, praise your dog so he knows that he has done well and leave the ring quietly and graciously. A congratulatory comment to the winner on the way out would be good etiquette.

Guard Dogs

Whenever guard dogs are mentioned the picture immediately comes to mind of salivating, snarling dogs throwing themselves against chain-link fences. This is not a guard dog but a scared dog. A properly trained guard dog is a quiet animal who knows the capability of his actions and has the confidence to know when to be aggressive (not vicious) and when to be quiet.

A good guard dog is a result of the correct type of training for the proper job by a person who knows the differences and can recognise the correct application. If this is a little confusing consider that the words 'guard dog' refer not to the Hollywood stereotype as described above but to four types of dogs: the alarm dog; the threat dog; the patrol dog and the man taker.

Any form of guard response by a dog is the present-day manifestation of the age-old instinct

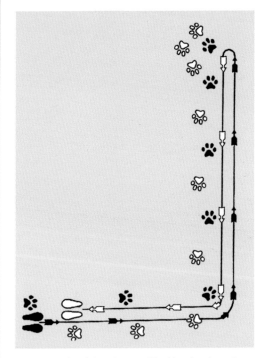

Moving the Bullmastiff.

L pattern (involving change of lead hand to keep dog between you and judge at all times).

to hunt. The primeval instinct to hunt is in all dogs. They show it by digging holes, chasing the cat, running after a ball or whatever; these are the remnants of the hunting instinct. When you train a dog to guard you sharpen an already inherent reaction. What should be borne in mind by the enthusiastic owner is the fact that when the wild dog did run loose and hunt for himself there were no such things as social responsibilities and by-laws. It is very easy to awaken this old instinct but it is more difficult to convince your dog that he must stop when you say. With this in mind, make haste slowly and, in whatever form of training, ensure that as you go you, rather than the dog's instinct, are the one in control.

The alarm dog

Almost any breed of dog can play the role of alarm dog. In this role the dog's only duty is to make as much noise as possible on hearing a stranger approach. Such a dog encourages any would-be thief to leave quickly before too much attention is drawn to his presence. The

Using the whole ring - including the corners - to move your dog.

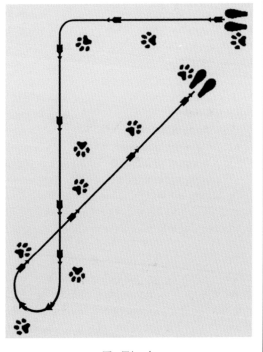

The Triangle.

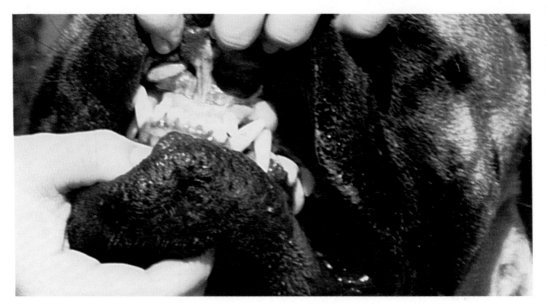

Showing the teeth for the judge's inspection. Be sure to expose clearly all the incisors and canines. Wide canines are a good indication of broadness of muzzle, so don't miss the opportunity to show this to your judge.

more noise the dog makes the more effective he is. If challenged the alarm dog will probably have no stomach for repelling the trespasser. This is not the dog's purpose; he is only required to make a noise and draw attention to his locality. It is easier for the interloper to go elsewhere than to risk being caught because of some yappy little dog.

Although the alarm type dogs are usually smaller breeds, the Bullmastiff fulfils this job quite well when the dog is younger. To add to his merits the young Bullmastiff is quite large and the breed relatively unknown. Such a mix would make any but the most stout-hearted back away, so if you want your Bullmastiff to be nothing more than this then teach him so.

The threat dog

This is the dog that most people refer to as a guard dog. He is the kind postmen are most likely to encounter on their rounds. The threat dog is normally a dog of sufficient size and stature to command respect from even the most daring of delivery agents. The dog's purpose is that of deterrence: to stand his ground whenever a stranger enters his property and challenge the presence of the newcomer with a growl, maybe showing his teeth by way of reinforcement.

It is not part of a threat dog's job to take up battle with the intruder, most of whom will take heed of the dog's attitude (especially if it belongs to one of the more publicised guard breeds) and leave quietly, allowing the dog to go back to sleep. If challenged the threat dog may submit to intimidation and back away to a more defensible position. Under most circumstances, however, the means and effect fulfil the owner's requirements: no one enters, and all involved play out their roles.

The Bullmastiff by birthright is a natural threat dog. His whole breed reasoning was dependent on his ability to guard an area such as your garden. His presence and appearance make a very good threat display even before that roll of thunder known as a growl emanates from deep inside him and rids your property of any unwanted person. This is your Bullmastiff's natural guarding tendency coming out as he matures. The level of response to such a situation depends on you, the owner. If you want this kind of guard dog, praise him to reinforce his actions after such an incident. Remember to curb a dog whose enthusiasm is a little too much if the threatening continues after the intruder has left. As stated before, bringing out that old instinct is easy; controlling it is another matter. Only reinforce as much as you can control; learning on the job that you have lost control can be detrimental to all involved. Until you do have control lock your gate, put up notices, and install a bell.

The patrol dog
Owners who employ Bullmastiffs as patrol guards for premises such as scrap yards, secure yards, or estates owe the breed a special measure of responsibility. The breed was originally bred to patrol a territory (the English estate) with a definite purpose in view. Using the Bullmastiff for this purpose draws on every original guarding fibre in the breed. Such a dog is not usually allowed to mix with other dogs, people or family. This results in a very protective, aggressive dog who makes

Thorneywood Terror, considered the most clever and highly trained dog of his time.

the four corners of the area his kingdom, his master's kingdom, with a readiness to defend against anyone foolish enough to jump the fence. You are calling on eons of genetics when you employ a dog such as this and very little true training is necessary except for the dog to recognise the handler/owner for feeding and kennelling purposes and for the owner initially to reinforce his defensive actions with words of praise. This is not the kind of dog to take to the park on a Sunday afternoon. Like a trained commando he has one purpose in life. Do not fail him by carelessness. Better still, buy another breed; Bullmastiffs are too special to be treated like this.

The man taker
This is the term applied to any breed of dog that is employed in some form of security situation specifically to apprehend a person. They are otherwise described as attack-trained, protection-trained, or whatever term is used to describe the awakened hunting instinct of a Bullmastiff to attack and hold a man.

Consider that a fully grown, mature male Bullmastiff in hard working condition may weigh 68kg (150lb), and a charging dog may reach 48km (30 miles) an hour. Imagine a man driving a car at that speed, hitting a tree, and stopping within a half a metre. In real life the tree is the quarry and, if you use the equation of

$$\frac{M \times V^2}{2}$$

(where M = dog's body mass and V = Velocity), the mechanical advantage to the moving dog equates to somewhere over four tonnes. This should indicate the amount of power involved when the Bullmastiff is used as an attack dog.

Bullmastiffs make excellent attack dogs and can deter even the most stout-hearted adversaries. They are tractable, responsive, trainable, with excellent retention, and can do the job well. Some who have had the dubious pleasure of acting as the agitator, the pretend bad-guy, have compared the sight of a charging Bullmastiff to that of a bulldozer with teeth.

A Bullmastiff uses its heavy wide chest to demolish the agitator and grab the protected arm offered to it. As a result of training, their instinct is to flatten and pin.

After apprehending an intruder in such a manner the same dog will play with your children like a soft lap dog, rolling, fawning, and enjoying all the privileges of the family pet. Conditioning of this sort requires knowledge, experience and a full understanding of the Bullmastiff, his psychological make-up and, most of all, a thorough working knowledge of such types of training.

The man taker: manwork in South Africa

In deference to the breed, and in recognition of the problems that could befall an enthusiastic novice, all such training should be referred to a professional. The new owner should not attempt this type of training except under the guidance of a reputable, knowledgeable, professional trainer.

Which Type of Training?

When you have decided which kind of training interests you, familiarise yourself with the whole programme before you start. There is nothing worse than a half-trained dog reacting in a new way with which the owner does not know how to cope because he has not read far enough in the training manual.

CHAPTER SEVEN

Breeding

S & N Cook's Bulltyron Zulu Dawn, eight weeks in whelp. The bitch becomes very cumbersome as delivery day approaches.

In every fancier's life there comes a time when the age old subject of breeding arises. Do you want puppies? Does your family? Does your dog? The question to be answered by all those involved is, 'Why?'

Do you feel all children should see puppies born at least once as a necessary lesson of life? If you want to show the miracle of birth to your family, buy white mice. The cycle is faster and repetitive and, when the kids tire of the miracle, a short trip to the pet store will remedy the loss of enthusiasm by all concerned.

So you think it is good for the dog. Who said it is? Your dog can undergo some serious personality changes during and after motherhood, and you might not like some of the changes you see, especially if they are permanent. If you enjoy your dog the way she is, leave her to be herself. Some people are under the false belief that a bitch must have puppies to fulfil her role as a female dog. Do you feel that all women must have children to be better women? The bitch's hormones can mature well enough without the miracle of motherhood.

How well the bitch responds to puppies, motherhood, the joy of cleaning up after her brood and all the rest of the maternal scene is a total unknown until the first time. Some bitches love it, some hate it. Remember you may have to play mother for at least four weeks if the bitch does not like her puppies. Like parenthood, breeding Bullmastiffs is a wonderful thing, but it has to be approached with thought, care and responsibility, and with the knowledge that every puppy will have an impact on the breed, no matter how small you may consider your part in it. Consider the implications of letting your bitch have puppies carefully before you take the irreversible step.

Finally, if you are responsible for eight or nine baby Bullmastiffs, will you also be responsible for finding a responsible owner for each one, or will you simply visit the pet shop or dogs' home to remedy the situation? Puppyhood is a state of life that must be approached, like any other living scenario, with care and careful consideration.

Do you want puppies to better and enhance the breed? You do? Good! Read on.

Choosing a Mate

There is no gain to the breed, the fancy, to Bullmastiffs in general or to the world if you breed only for the sake of producing puppies. Go ahead only if you are breeding to enhance the breed. There are many 'back street' breeders who harm many breeds of dog each year by producing purely for monetary gain without any thought of the future of the breed. When the breed in which they are dabbling is ruined by such irresponsibility, they move on to another. Many self-authorised 'experts' will buy a female Bullmastiff and proceed to breed her to every well-known dog in the country. The unscrupulous dealer seeks to justify this by claiming that his or her line will have all the best of each dog in it, but it is a clear case of genetic irresponsibility.

Without wishing to give you a comprehensive lesson in genetics, it is sufficient to say that Bullmastiffs with similar characteristics who are mated together will reinforce those characteristics in the breed by producing them in their pups. As all of their characteristics may not be totally similar, the inherited characteristic in the pups will be decided by whichever dog has the strongest gene in that particular area. This might be called a genetic compromise. By breeding together dogs with similar backgrounds the breeder has a fair idea of what to expect in his litter. Certain grey areas will always remain and will depend on the genetic struggle; the results will be seen in the litter as slightly different physical characteristics (phenotype). The breeder can only calculate and guess the genetic bundle (genotype) that each dog carries in his genes by his knowledge of the dog's pedigree.

Outcrossing

No matter how minimal your understanding of genetics you will see that, when two dogs have no similarities other than being Bullmastiffs, no-one can accurately forecast the characteristics of their puppies. This method is called straight outcrossing and it is a very risky way of breeding if carried out carelessly. The breeder can ruin all the years of selective line breeding by previous breeders, treating their work as if their cares and struggles were worth nothing. He has to be aware of the endless variations that can be produced when this action is done thoughtlessly. The variations in type that this produces could take the breed back to the 19th century.

There is one time when a breeder would be forgiven for showing this kind of apparent disdain. This is when he is aware of the prepotency of the two dogs and wants to see if his calculated guess will produce the dog that he, as a breeder, has sought over many years.

Prepotency
Each one of us has certain characteristics that we attribute to our ancestors. It might be the colour of our eyes, our stature, or even our height. These kinds of dominant physical characteristics are prepotencies. Dogs are just as prepotent as we are and, after many breedings of one particular dog, a breeder will know which characteristics are prepotent to his dog. For instance, if dog A is prepotent in heads, and dog B is prepotent in muzzles, the chances are that when dog A is bred to dog B the puppies will have the heads of dog A and the muzzles of dog B. However, nature has a way of overriding all our calculations on prepotency when she feels like it.

Breeding programme
In some cases the prepotency packages cannot all be put together in one breeding and may have to be done gradually over many years with many dogs in what is referred to as a breeding programme. In some cases nature is co-operative and the package comes together easily. In others it may take 20 years. It depends on what is required, what is available, and the breeder's intent in relation to the standard.

Sometimes hours of looking at pedigrees is the only way to work out a breeding programme. Many long-time breeders will know the characteristics of old lines and their knowledge will easily outweigh hours of paper theory. Information like this is worth its weight in gold, so do not spurn it. Conversely, remember that individual prejudices and preferences will often affect judgement so be sure you are listening to the right person.

If your knowledge of Bullmastiffs is limited and you have not seen other Bullmastiffs, take a trip to another area and familiarise yourself. Video cameras can sometimes save you the cost of a trip if the fancier you choose to contact is co-operative.

Take time to research honestly long before you have need of a mate for your dog. One of the best people to talk to is the breeder of your own dog. Since you bought your Bullmastiff from the breeder because you liked it better than the others you saw, the chances are that you appreciated your breeder's programme. He will be knowledgeable about his dogs' lines and the prepotencies of your dog and will recommend a mate. He can tell you what you might expect in your litter.

Line breeding
In general terms line breeding occurs when both parents have similar dogs in their background. This allows the pairing of similar genetic packages and guarantees certain characteristics in your litter. The dissimilar ones are usually less significant and can often be calculated by noting the prepotencies of previous litters. In pairing genetic packages, the pairing strengthens prepotencies, and will do so even if the prepotency is not a good one (for example, straight shoulder). Once it is strengthened a stronger genetic package will be needed to break through it.

In-breeding
This occurs when dogs within the same line are bred to each other (for example, father to daughter or mother to son). In some cases this can produce excellent dogs; however, in most cases it is a genetic disaster. Prior to such a venture the breeder must be completely aware of each and every characteristic, good and bad, of the line involved and be honest about the outcome. If the litter proves to be a bad one the breeder must take the responsibility of culling it to ensure inferior dogs do not influence the generations of Bullmastiffs yet to come.

Colour breeding

Colour consideration should be a concern of a breeder when he attempts to produce a litter. The standard states that the colour should be clear, and this clear colour does not appear or remain by accident or chance. The colour of your Bullmastiff is a delicate blend of the main colour, whether it is red or fawn, and a subtle application of pigment. In the brindle this shows as stripes to provide the camouflage colouring, in the reds and fawns it shows as the darkness in the ears, nose, eye shading, nails and, in all cases, a black mask.

The early breeders were quick to realise that continual breeding of red to red, or fawn to fawn, weakened the dominant colour and allowed the darker pigment to show through in the form of dark pencilling over the entire body of the dog, reducing the clearness to a muddy, unacceptable colour. This occurred when the pigment which provides the colour in a brindle, but remains recessive except in deliberate brindle breeding, was allowed to become stronger than the dominant colour by constant line or inbreeding to the same colour.

Owing to the origin of the Bullmastiff lineage, few Bullmastiff lines can claim a brindle-free line. It is this brindling that provides the necessary paint pot to strengthen the colour combination. As brindle is recessive in the Bullmastiff, breeding to a brindle will allow the mixing of the dominant colour genes to strengthen the colour while the brindle colour itself remains recessive in a red or fawn dog. The same effect would be achieved if a red dog that was a product of many generations of line breeding in that colour was bred to an outcross red dog for colour strengthening. The variations of different Bullmastiff types, as previously discussed, would be another consideration, but for colour this would do the trick.

It is interesting to note that to produce a normal brindle Bullmastiff litter one of the parents has to be brindle. Although there are a few known exceptions to this rule, the norm is no brindle parent, no brindle litter. If a comparison is made of the pigmentation and strength of colour in a brindle litter it will be clearly seen that the quality of colour as compared to that of a line that does not attempt to use the brindle ink pot is far superior.

Take a look at your Bullmastiff, making a mental note of the type of dog you would like to produce. Then, as if you were a genetic engineer, take the necessary steps. Producing life is a wonderful thing and seeing those new-born puppies snuggling up to their mother is a sight to soften the hardest heart. But remember, if you are responsible for that litter, be proud of it, now and forever.

Mating – The Easy Way

Like everything else in life, there is an easy way and a hard way. Considering the size, weight, and disposition of this large breed it is not hard to see it could be quite problematic trying to manoeuvre two very large dogs, sometimes as big as their owners, into cooperating in a way that might not be agreeable to them at that particular time, for whatever reasons. The attempt can result in two very tired handlers full of frustration, and no chance of conception in sight. The following section provides the novice with a proven and tried method of breeding Bullmastiffs in a way known to be successful and relatively easy. As the proverb says: 'When all else fails, read these instructions'.

The only aim in mating is to allow the semen of the male to fertilise the ova of the female. No matter how you put it the outcome is the same the whole world over and in every culture. The action is as basic as life itself and anyone engaging in this age-old ritual has to accept this fact before proceeding any further. To this end the following chapter is explicit, comprehensive and explains everything you wanted to know about canine sex but were afraid to ask.

There are two ways of connecting the semen to the ova successfully: artificially, otherwise known as artificial insemination (AI), and the natural, physical way. The only right way is the way that results in conception; the choice of method will depend on the owner of the bitch or the agreement of contract between the owners of the two dogs involved.

Long before either method is used the owner of the bitch should have determined within a reasonable time when the bitch is due to come into heat. Some bitches show a lot of swelling and discolouration of the vulva when heat approaches, others can be so discreet that, unless the owner is watching, the bitch can sneak in and out of heat and not give her secret away. The usual signs of heat are fussiness, during which the bitch licks and cleans herself profusely, and the need to urinate often. However, instead of stooping and emptying her bladder normally, the bitch mimics the male action and leaves little drops everywhere to attract males. She will inevitably leave blood spots around. Some bitches show a lot, some very little, so beware of being fooled by a bitch that appears not to be in heat.

As soon as this starts it will be as well to pay a visit to your veterinary surgeon. Unless you know your bitch well you may not be able to catch the first day of oestrus accurately. It is very important to determine the day of ovulation or your efforts at breeding will be wasted. The day of ovulation varies from dog to dog and the only way to be sure of it the first time is to study cells from your bitch's uterus that have been discharged by her as she enters her heat period. Your vet will take a vaginal smear and stain and check it under the microscope to see how far into the heat she is.

If you are unable to take your bitch to the vet it may be necessary to take your own smears and forward these to the veterinary laboratory for study. The vet will provide the necessary blank slides for you to use. Scratch your fingernail into the frosted area at the one end of the slide. One side will mark, the other will not. Use the side of the slide which marks. The name and other details of the dog can be marked into the frosted area for record purposes.

The best time to take the smear is first thing in the morning. You will need two cotton swabs, and someone to hold the bitch's head. Open the lips of her vulva wide and insert the head of the cotton swab into the vagina as far as you can without feeling resistance. It is important that the swab does not touch the external sides of the vulva as it will be contaminated with debris and old cells that have dried out from some time before. At this point of the proceedings the swab will be suitably coated with cells that have descended her vagina from her uterus. You may not be able to see anything on the swab except a little moistness, or maybe a little pinkness, but this is a good sample. Keep the vulva lips wide open, withdraw the swab and roll the swab to leave a deposit on one edge of the slide. Perform this procedure again with a new swab and place the second deposit alongside the first (see diagram on following page). Note that both these samples are on the same side of the slide.

Having done this, immediately take the slide firmly at its edges and shake it rapidly in the air. This will dry the mucous that accompanies the cells to make them stick firmly to the glass of the slide.

This slide can now be put into an envelope without fear of losing the smear. It is a good idea to mark the date and name of the dog on the slide. If you take numerous slides this dating will assist your records.

Once the laboratory technician has analysed the slide some idea of the bitch's cycle stage can be determined. Depending on the stage your vet may require more slides. He will instruct you on their frequency and necessity. Ultimately he will tell you when the bitch is due to ovulate. This is the optimum time of conception and usually the only time the bitch willingly accepts the male's attention to completion of mating. However, as most bitches vary, only time will tell. Some breeders prefer to better the odds by performing an artificial insemination (AI) prior to the true ovulation date and completing the mating naturally if possible at the correct time. If the bitch is uncooperative to the male or refuses to accept him, further AIs may be necessary. This is the decision of those involved in the breeding and differs from dog to dog and mating to mating; time and experience help you to assess the situation.

Unless both owners are extremely experienced and know their dogs very well, one thing that should never be done is what many laymen think breeding is all about: to turn both dogs into a room or pen as if they were cattle, 'leave them to it', and come back half an hour later expecting nature to have taken its course. Sometimes this has been known to work. If you are willing to risk your dog being injured for life, badly scarred from fighting owing to an unwilling bitch refusing a very determined male, or so traumatised from an aggressive response it will never mate again, go ahead. These are big dogs with a lot of weight, size, and big powerful jaws that are quick to respond at times like this. Don't risk it!

Artificial Insemination

Many breeders prefer this approach all the time as it avoids physical contact and transmission of many diseases, and allows the breeder to determine the time and the quality and amount of sperm, and to have control of the whole procedure.

In Great Britain puppies produced by artificial insemination will be registered by The Kennel Club only if previous permission has been granted by its General Council. Detailed reasons will be required for using this method and the correct application form for permission must be completed and returned by the breeder. The method is very seldom used in Great Britain for the home breeding programme, although frozen semen from leading sires in various breeds has been exported. The kennel clubs of many countries now register puppies conceived by this method and, where British stock is concerned, it obviates the period of quarantine that would be necessary in the case of a natural mating. Mr Price of the Lombardy affix makes the following comments:

> *...artificial insemination is very seldom used here, in fact it would require the permission of The Kennel Club. Perhaps this is because there are no great distances to travel, so natural matings are easier and cheaper. Although we have world class facilities for insemination of cattle, none exist specifically for dogs.*
>
> *Natural matings are always used at Lombardy. My method is to go by the colour of the bitch's discharge: a simple swab is easily done by anyone. When this is colourless the bitch is ready – usually around the 14th day of the season.*

I feel that the female should always be taken to the male. Never take your male to the female's home as there will be so many wonderful female odours to investigate he will lose time, interest and possibly stamina from all the hormone excitement. There again, where great distances are involved, a bitch upset by the journey may have her ovulation postponed, but it will come eventually; a dog's sperm count may be so adversely affected by stress that he will be unable to sire puppies.

Prior to any interaction between the two candidates clinical protocol must be observed. The genital areas of both animals must be cleaned with an antiseptic solution to avoid the cross-transmission of bacterial infections or any other communicable diseases.

Some males need the presence of the female to initiate erection. If this is so allow the male to acquaint himself with the rear end of the female and the odorous discharge will bring his attention into line. Other males can be initiated into erection if you depress the nerves found behind the bulbous area at the base of the penis. If depression is insufficient a pulsation of the area will always create the simulation of the pulsing of the female's sphincter muscle at a rate of 0.8 per second; it is around this area that the female's sphincter muscle grasps and pulsates during natural copulation.

Once erection is accomplished the semen will soon flow, the male's

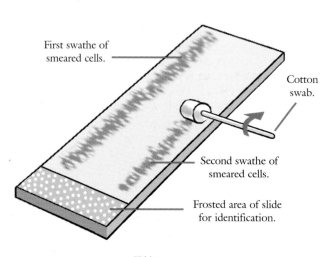

First swathe of smeared cells.

Cotton swab.

Second swathe of smeared cells.

Frosted area of slide for identification.

Taking a smear.

pulsations also occurring at 0.8 per second. If the penis is grasped at the base behind the bulbous area this action will simulate the muscular action of the female and maintain erection. Experience and scrutiny will tell the operator when it is time to finish collection of the semen. The first 30–60 seconds of emission usually contain old and inactive semen. The second portion (times may overlap) at approximately 50–80 seconds is the sample that will contain the necessary motile semen. After that, the ejaculated fluid is that of lubricant, mostly from the prostate gland and almost clear in colour in comparison to the whiter, denser colour of the true semen.

The collection vessel can be anything from a large medical syringe to a glass sterilised beforehand and allowed to come to room temperature before use, assuming room temperature is about 24°C (75°F). Once collected the semen will cool quickly and must be administered to the female as soon as possible. Do not bang the vessel as canine semen is very fragile and a bump can kill your sample and make any further action that time futile. At this time some breeders prefer to check the motility and count of the sample by using a slide and a small droplet from the vessel to assure themselves all is well with the male if the bitch does not conceive.

For a Bullmastiff an open-ended catheter similar to the kind used for horses or cows is ideal for depositing the semen. Administering is made easier if the catheter is cut to approximately 20cm (8in) and the end is flamed to round it and remove any straight or rough edges. To this attach a 20cc syringe and carefully withdraw the sample from the vessel. A good sample to give a reasonable chance of conception would be 10–15cc. Do not withdraw the plunger of the syringe any further when all the sample has been removed from the vessel. One thing not required in the vagina is air.

Be sure you have enough assistance to prevent the bitch's head from turning towards you for obvious reasons, and have someone hold her tail out of the way. The bitch's vagina does not connect with the outside world in a straight continuous line so be prepared for this. As you enter the catheter into the vulva you will be aware that the vagina rises slightly and is sometimes partially blocked by a flap of membrane. Careful manoeuvring of the catheter will negotiate this membrane and the bend in the vagina and the catheter can then be inserted fully.

An alternate method is to grasp the lower portion of the vulva and pull it up and straight out towards you. This will bring the vagina into a straight line and therefore assist in the insertion of the catheter. If the thumb of the free hand is inserted into the vagina to act as a guide for the incoming catheter it will assist the initial insertion and also ensure that the tip of the catheter does not hang up in the entrance to the urinary tract (urethra). At this stage of heat there will be no objection from the female as everything will be soft and pliable in the genital area. The action must be slow, sensitive, and with the syringe held in such a way that any sudden rear movement or rejection by the bitch will allow the syringe and catheter to fall away from her, in no way threatening to perforate her vaginal wall. The internal end of the catheter will be round, bulbous, and wide so movement internally will not be unpleasant, but precautions must be taken against every possible scenario.

If the vagina seems resistant to the insertion movements or you believe you have reached the furthest point of deposition, slightly withdraw the catheter and eject a small quantity of the semen. If the problem is lubrication the small emission will assist the continuing procedure; if not you will know that the point of deposition has been reached. Sometimes when the catheter goes easily the end wall of the vagina is soon reached. However, when the plunger is depressed, a resistance is noticed due to the fact that the soft tissue at the end of the vagina has completely sealed off the end of the catheter. Then, as with the lubrication problem, a slight withdrawal will cure the situation and the plunger can be depressed.

Now is the important time of deposition. Depress the plunger slowly and evenly until the syringe is empty. If you withdraw the catheter at this time you will siphon out quite a large amount of the semen by the displacement effect of the catheter. Therefore remove the syringe from the catheter and quickly place your thumb over the open end of the catheter to avoid leakage, withdraw the plunger of the syringe about 2cc and re-connect to the catheter. Remembering that you do not want air in the vagina, depress the syringe plunger slowly at the same time as you withdraw the

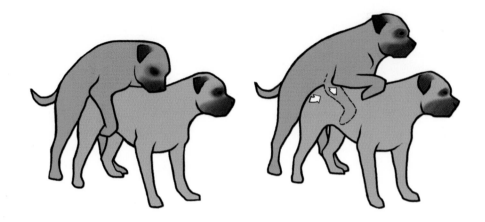

syringe and catheter from the vagina. This allows the maximum amount of semen to stay where it should with the minimum loss. In case the bitch coughs, barks, or moves suddenly pinch the lips of the vulva together to avoid loss of semen and possible ruination of your AI. If it is possible try to raise the rear end of the bitch off the floor by whatever method is available for approximately five minutes.

If you can negotiate the little finger of the hand through the lips of the vulva and apply pressure to the bitch's clitoris, the natural pulsation of 0.8 per second can be produced in the vaginal sphincter muscle, assisting the semen along its natural course. Do not allow the bitch to urinate for 20 minutes.

This concludes the breeding by AI. Depending on the arrangement between the two owners of the parent dogs, this may be all that's involved. Further breedings will depend on the ambient breeding protocol or contract terms.

Natural Breeding

Natural breeding is very aclinical. It presents a very different scene from AI, when all genital contact areas such as vulva and penis sheath are clean and comparatively sterile and free from transmissible infection. For the purpose of this section, we will assume that both bitch and dog are novices at breeding.

The genital areas of both dogs should be checked for cleanliness. If in doubt wash the genitals with an aseptic solution.

Some male dogs' senses are very acute and the presence of a bitch in heat is obvious to them. However, some bitches, no matter how much in heat, need to check out the sex of the dog approaching them. Both dogs should be secure on leads to allow a sensory introduction on both their parts. It will serve to assure the bitch that this really is a male approaching her, and it will heighten the male's sexual acuity. Many males would be satisfied with a headlong rush and rape at first sight. Such a blundering approach will only serve to scare or intimidate a nervous bitch into total refusal to mate. An experienced bitch will know what to expect and often put up with much more roughness than a maiden bitch. If not controlled by the handler, inexperienced males will often rush at the bitch too quickly and ejaculate prematurely, thus ruining all chances of a successful mating. After numerous breedings the handlers of the bitch and dog both know what to expect and so the necessary adjustments to control can be made to suit the occasion.

Some breeders like to allow their dogs to run around and get to know each other before actual mating starts. Once again this is fine if you know your dogs well. However, if the male gets too amorous too soon for the bitch's liking the romantic frolic can soon turn sour. Depending on the mood of the bitch, this can be so quick and sudden that it may be impossible to prevent this. The

Manoeuvring the dogs during the tie.

way your Bullmastiff reacts under such conditions may show you a side of your dog you have not hitherto encountered in your gentle family pet.

Be prepared and be safe; do not let your dog or yourself get bitten because of romantic reversions. Keep your dog on the lead even when allowing the pair to flirt. This way if courtship takes a wrong turn you can intervene before it gets serious and the mating will not be affected.

For the safety of the male who will be preoccupied in mounting the female without any thought for his personal safety, the female's head should be held tightly forward. This prevents her turning and biting the male's face should she not appreciate his physical endeavours. If her head is held tightly it will also ensure her body stays in line with her head. In case she does happen to swing around it is useful to have a third party present to move her back into position.

The male should be allowed to approach her slowly, not with a rush; careful manipulation with the lead will produce this effect. The male will mount from the back and commence the hip movement associated with copulation. At this point the movement is voluntary and controlled and he may dismount and restart more than once. At this time the tip of the penis has not come into contact with the vulva and remains quite small. However, once the end of the penis has encountered the vulva opening, involuntary muscular thrusts will occur as the vulva creates pressure on the penis. It is of the greatest importance that the male's genitals are as close to the female's as possible at this point to ensure maximum penetration. In a novice dog that is too far from the female it may be necessary for the handler to assist quickly by pushing the rear end of the dog closer to the female with a timely forward movement of his knee.

This will ensure the penetration necessary to place the bulbous area inside the female vaginal sphincter muscle. This action is necessary to ensure a tie. If the bulbous area of the penis enlarges outside the sphincter muscle the bitch may be able to prevent his total withdrawal by gripping his penis, but failure to tie will lead ultimately to the dog's premature withdrawal and possible failure of the mating and conception. The importance of this physical closeness at the time of the thrusting cannot be stressed enough. If the male is a little nervous and becomes frustrated when no penetration is achieved, his handler may need to assist by gently guiding the male's penis to the entrance of the vulva. Once physical contact is made the natural reactions will take over.

If a tie occurs the dogs may be locked together for 15 minutes or more as the male cannot withdraw until ejaculation is complete and the bulbous area subsides. Once he has tied successfully he will often appear to lose interest, although in his physical position he cannot go anywhere. Most males will naturally step down from the mounted position with their front legs to one side or the other of the female. A Bullmastiff's great weight is unbearable for most females and so, if he is a little slow at this or appears to be quite content where he is, assist him with his dismount. He cannot dismount without sliding one of his elbows over the top of the female's back. This can often prove to be quite a physical feat for a handler who has an uncooperative male. However once the elbow passes the peak of the female's back his weight will ensure a quick dismount. This will leave him standing with his forequarters alongside the female. Most pairs will take this opportunity to lick each other fondly but some may remain quite hostile.

To avoid potential problems it is wiser to turn the dogs so they are end to end. The secret in the turning at this point is not the elbow but the male's stifle, or knee. If he has dropped down onto her right it is his left stifle (knee) you will be manipulating. Bend the male's stifle by grasping the hock and push the knee over the female's back and at the same time pull his head in the opposite direction to the female's. The leg will naturally drop down and, with a little manoeuvring, the dogs will be end to end. At delicate moments you may hear a little complaining by the female, but as long as you move slowly and take care that their tails are out of the way, no harm will come to either.

During the tie either or both dogs may appear to lose interest in the proceedings and attempt to dissolve the partnership. Sometimes the female will try to sit down, or the male to walk off. To avoid physical damage to either, both handlers should make themselves comfortable on stools and hold the dogs in the end-to-end position. The dogs should be supervised in this fashion until the tie is over.

Once the tie is over the male will disconnect from the female and be more interested in his toiletries than in the female, who will be glad to be taken away quietly. With a little self cleaning the male's penis should resume normal proportions and withdraw safely to the protection of its sheath.

On rare occasions the erection will have been so excessive that the sheath impinges the blood vessels and does not allow the penis to withdraw. Application of a cold, wet cloth in the area will normally facilitate the required reduction. If this does not happen and there is no sign of normality returning accompanied by distress from your male, contact your vet quickly. Failure to do so may be serious to your dog's future breeding capabilities.

After the tie has broken the male will attend to himself, then look for a drink of water and a place to rest. This rest is important for both animals if healthy breeding stock is to be maintained. Fewer problems of stress and weight maintenance will be noticed if the two animals involved are housed well away from each other during the breeding time.

If there is a size disparity between the two animals it may be necessary to provide assistance to overcome this. If the dog's back legs are shorter than the bitch's, standing her in a shallow hole or with a roll of carpet behind her hocks will compensate for the difference. Conversely, if she is shorter, you may have to stand her on a wedge of carpet. In either case any possible chance of slipping by either dog must be avoided. Make sure the carpet or whatever is used provides good traction for the back feet.

Mr Price has the following comment on mating:

"Possibly because I have always had good stud dogs, I have experienced no difficulty in handling and achieving a mating single-handed; in fact I have used other people's dogs just as easily.

It is a simple process to hold the bitch firmly and steadily with one arm just in front of the back legs, leaving the other hand free to help and hold the dog as they mate and tie. Most dogs will drop down to the far side of the bitch and stand or turn whichever way they have been trained. I repeat the mating in 48 hours; there is no object in mating daily. Though I can manage this on my own it is helpful for the bitch's owner to sit on a chair and hold her head between his or her legs".

When the stud is well trained and the breeder experienced I would agree with this; in fact it is the method I use with my own dogs, who have been trained what to do from puppyhood. However, it can be a different matter in the case of dogs raised as pets who have no idea what is expected of them and resent any interference, especially in the case of larger animals. Bullmastiffs in Great Britain do tend to be smaller than those in other parts of the world (as reflected in the breed standards) which possibly would make them easier to mate.

Care of the Bitch after Mating

Your bitch has just been mated and you are hopeful of a litter. How you handle the female in the next two months will decide just how successful that is to be.

After the mating take your female away and put her somewhere peaceful and, if possible, private. You need to keep her quiet and subdued; any undue excitement such as meeting another bitch face to face or a cat that needs to be investigated can ruin your chances of success.

A confined area such as a crate is preferable and be sure she does not urinate for at least 20 minutes. The urge in female dogs in oestrus to do this as an advertisement to males is extremely strong. If she does this after mating the siphoning action can cause her to lose all the valuable semen you have just spent time acquiring. A quiet time for your bitch will be most suitable no matter how long you think fertilisation takes.

Depending on your arrangement with the owner of the stud further matings may be in the offing on successive nights. One thing to be wary of is too many matings too far apart. If a bitch who has conceived on the first mating is then mated four times on alternate nights any puppy conceived on a later night will be born at the same time as the first night puppy. This could be detrimental to the puppy conceived later. Repeat matings are fine but not too many and not too far apart. A good breeding would be three times on alternate nights. If the weather is hot it may be wiser to breed them at night anyway, especially if a brindle is involved, because dark dogs absorb heat at a tremendous rate. Breeding on a hot summer's day could be debilitating for both dogs.

The bitch will be attractive to other males for a total period of three weeks. Although she has been bred to a dog of your choice, she is not concerned with moral issues; nor are any roving males. Be sure she is well protected from any advances, either to her or from her. Quite often even a 2m (6ft) fence is not sufficient deterrent, so take all precautions. The only safe solution may be to crate her when she is not under direct supervision. Her attraction will not cease until the end of her heat cycle when the odour from her vaginal discharge ends. At this time a good bath and grooming will remove any residual smell that might attract unwelcome canine suitors. Do not forget the bedding and the living quarters. Maybe you know it is over but the residual smell will call all prospective fathers from miles around.

If she has conceived, physical changes soon start to show. Appetite is often the first indicator: all of a sudden the food intake increases dramatically. This is a good sign, but do not let your dog eat gluttonously and become overweight, as this will affect the correct working of other organs.

The nipples of an unbred bitch are usually flat and pinched. After breeding, hormone activity tends to swell the nipples so that they are plump and pink after conception, usually showing a difference the day after mating. Although not 100% accurate as a sign of conception it is more often right than wrong. A Bullmastiff is very muscular and the litter may not be evident until about the fifth week. It is at this time that the girth muscles seem to start giving up and the thickness of her rotundity can be observed. By this time her increase in appetite will have warned you well in advance of her condition and your vet will recommend when to start supplementing her food.

In the latter weeks take great care to make sure she does not jump up or down on anything, causing her to stretch the abdominal area of her body. This can cause severe movement of the puppies in the uterus horns and problems at birth. As the pressure mounts within her be aware that the pressure on her bladder means she needs to urinate frequently, and do not get impatient as she asks to go outside yet again.

The milk glands on the female's underside will begin to show like corded ropes, and traces of milk may become evident if the nipples are squeezed. As she gets heavier and more cumbersome, walking and general manoeuvring will become an effort, so do not hurry her. Be prepared to make allowances. She is big, heavy, often irritated, and probably wishing it was all over.

Although she is gravid, most fanciers would be amazed at the rate of response this rather turgid female can muster when she or her family are threatened. There is nothing more awesome than an almost full-term female Bullmastiff coming around in a defensive rush, so make sure she does not have to respond like this.

Whelping to Weaning

The Bullmastiff bitch becomes a very cumbersome and ungainly animal as the day approaches for her to whelp the pups. Birth usually occurs approximately 63 days after conception, although this can alter by a few days depending on the individual dog. If you are unsure a quick visit to your vet at about the 60-day mark may better prepare you for the actual day.

Because bitches seem to choose the most inadequate places in which to have puppies it is better for man and beast if your female is confined to a whelping box for the duration of the birth and a short while afterwards. Most pets object to being confined in one area when they are used to being with members of the family all the time; however for the benefit of the puppies, her own safety, and control of the situation, a whelping box is the more suitable alternative to chaos.

The whelping box

The most useful type of whelping box serves initially as a whelping area and afterwards as a puppy box until the puppies are about four weeks old. In dimensions it is 120cm x 120cm (4ft x 4ft). A piece of plywood raised off the floor serves well, the raised area preventing cold or dampness coming up through the bottom. It is often better to leave this 'floor' unfinished except for the scantiest covering of newspaper. It should either be natural wood or wood painted in such a way that there will be adequate traction for the puppies. This avoids any covering being piled up and perhaps a puppy suffocating as a result of a well-meaning mother nesting and inadvertently covering it over. A newspaper covering is cheap and convenient, and any soiled material can be quickly removed as events proceed. The sides of the whelping box are made from a full piece of 120cm x 240cm (4ft x 8ft) plywood cut into four strips, each 60cm x 120cm (2ft x 4ft). These strips form the walls of the whelping box on three sides. On the fourth side, the strip is cut again to give two pieces of plywood 30cm x 120cm (1ft x 4ft). These two pieces are hinged to each other on the 120cm edge and attached on one of the 120cm edges to the floor on the partially completed whelping box. The hinged part that is free allows one side to be lowered to allow the bitch to come and go as her owner desires. During times of complete confinement or whelping, the hinged part can be raised and the whelping box made secure.

A most important part of the whelping equipment is the heat lamp. This can take the form of a chick brooder bulb with a protective safety cage around it or a heating panel as used in pig rearing. Either can be used successfully to create a floor temperature of 30°C (85°F) for the first week. This allows the puppies to stay warm enough to ward off herpes, pneumonia, or any other infection to which they may be vulnerable when the mother is not present to keep them at the right temperature. For the first days of life the puppies rely on you and your heating lamp, or their mother, to control their body temperature; their natural thermostats will not be functioning yet. This temperature can be gradually lowered to 24°C (75°F) after a week. This extra thought will allow the mother a little freedom from her maternal chores as the pups will not immediately miss her when she leaves the box and takes her body heat with her. If the heat is aimed in such a way as to cover only one half of the whelping box the mother will often lie out of the heat path, but the puppies will be snug and warm.

One final structure in the whelping box and everything is ready: this is the crush rail. During whelping, and just after, the presence of puppies may not be obvious or of concern to a first-time mother. Occasionally the bitch will lie down suddenly and onto the puppies. After a short while she learns to slide down and push any puppies in the way out of her lying area, so causing no harm. However, in the early days precautions have to be taken to ensure the litter's safety. The crush rail consists of a wooden rail 5cm x 5cm (2in x 2in) running around the inside of the whelping box approximately 15cm (6in) off the floor and 30cm (12in) from the walls. This can be further enhanced by blocking out the corners in the box and presenting a floor area that will not allow puppies to become squashed into any corner but always in a position to claim mother's attention. In the first few days of life puppies react to stimulus such as heat and pain by crying, but cannot move away, so all possibilities have to be considered in designing the whelping box.

It helps if the whelping box becomes the bitch's home about two weeks before the litter is due. This overcomes her objections in plenty of time and allows her to settle down to normal living before the babies arrive. Place the whelping box in a quiet, well lit, warm, draught-free area where she can have privacy when the time comes but also in a position that gives you easy access when you want.

Labour

Prior to whelping, the bitch indulges in a great deal of excessive action: frantic nest building, asking to go out to urinate, panting, and general restlessness. A sure sign that puppies are imminent is the failure to eat her meal. Up to this time she usually eats ravenously but the day of the birth most mothers-to-be cover over their meal and want no part of it. This is the time to prepare a small puppy-holding box and line it with a clean towel and a heating pad. Set the heat control on low. If the puppy becomes too hot his feet and abdomen will go bright pink or purple. The puppies will cry if they get too cold, but too much heat may result in brain damage and a dead puppy.

View of the whelping box with hinged flap down to allow observation of pups and access by bitch.

Whelping

As the birth begins, strong muscular contractions will be seen in the stomach area. There will be some false starts when she will stop straining and sleep or look around uninterestedly. However, once the serious pushing begins, puppies are on the way. Do not allow her to strain and strain when nothing seems to be happening, certainly for no more than three hours. If your dog is in obvious distress contact your vet. It is a good idea to have pre-warned him or her of your possible middle-of-the-night appeal.

In most cases a puppy will appear head first. Do not be distressed if you see your puppy appearing bottom first (breach birth). This is quite common in this breed and most bitches have little problem delivering a breach. Should the puppy be an exceptionally big one and the breach presentation render whelping even more difficult, you may have to help. With clean hands, preferably washed in a clinical soap, or failing that with a clean piece of cloth, grasp the rear legs of the half-born puppy. As you feel the mother contract and push, pull gently but firmly. You will be very aware when this happens once you have hold of the puppy. When the bitch stops straining, you stop pulling. Do not try to pull the puppy out between contractions; go with the flow.

Problems like this do not occur too often and usually you can sit and just watch. Depending when the placenta actually detaches, the puppy may have sufficient oxygen to maintain him until the mother breaks the membrane and clears the airways. Sometimes a new mother is confused as to what to do first. Lost time in clearing the membrane may lose you a puppy so reach over and break the membrane around the mouth of the puppy with your fingers; it is very important to get that first breath as soon as possible. The rush of fluid usually stimulates the mother to react and her vigorous licking and pushing stimulates the puppy to breathe and wriggle, hence causing more breathing. Sometimes a mother will be so concerned at removing the afterbirth from herself or the puppy, she will momentarily forget the puppy. The whole point of this exercise is to end up with a live litter and this procedure ensures live puppies regardless of your bitch's attitude. A piece of dry cloth will help you grasp the puppy.

Once the puppy is fully born, quietly reach over and snip the umbilical cord with sharp surgical (round nosed) scissors about 1 inch from the pup's stomach and deftly remove the puppy. The bitch will often be so preoccupied with her toiletries she will not notice. Quickly slip some thread around the severed cord and tie tightly about 1.25cm (0.5in) from the puppy's abdomen, sealing off the umbilical. Now comes the tricky part. Hold the puppy in your two hands so that your index fingers run along the sides of the puppy's mouth and the finger tips are just inside the mouth. Holding this package very tightly raise the puppy above your head and bring your arms down as fast as you can without letting go of your charge. The resultant centrifugal force of this action will eject all of the fluid out of the puppy's lungs and throat and ensure a clear airway.

Some people do not like to take the centrifugal approach except in emergencies. Experience has shown that the deep chest and lungs and the presentation of the puppy at birth nearly always means it has a lot of fluid in the lungs and throat. The swing action ensures the lungs are free and clear and the shock of this to the puppy is a lot less distressing than lying gurgling with fluid in the lungs. If you see the puppy is distressed when it is removed from the mother, a quicker approach is to attach forceps to the severed umbilical, lie the forceps along the body of the puppy (which are held tightly alongside his body) and proceed to the swing immediately. Many apparently dead or dying puppies have been saved this way. Watch the tongue; as long as it is pink there is hope.

These actions will cause the puppy to cry out, and sometimes the mother becomes very upset with the person causing this apparent harm to her baby. For this reason you must be ready to return the puppy to his mother quickly. If you present the puppy towards the bitch with your hands behind and under it she will be so glad to see her pup she will forget the cry of distress and be only too pleased to get her baby back.

At this time the bitch will be lavishing all kinds of motherly love on her pup in the form of

licking, cleaning, general cleaning-up and eating the afterbirth. If the mother is not too lavish with her licks of life, help out by briskly rubbing the pup's stomach and lung area with a wet, rough face cloth (a dry one burns the skin because of the friction). As soon as you can, make sure the puppy nurses, even if you have to force an unwilling mouth open and over a nipple. It is of extreme importance that the puppy has a measure of the colostrum in the first milk, which passes the bitch's immunity to the pup. Once the puppy has nursed, or if another puppy is imminent, remove the

Ch Shayla's Bonni during whelping, cleaning up a puppy.

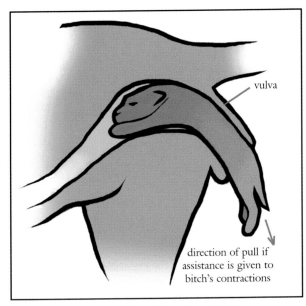

vulva

direction of pull if
assistance is given to
bitch's contractions

Assisting the bitch during a breach birth.

puppy to his warming box. A towel over the box will prevent heat loss. Once the puppy has nursed he will be quite happy to settle down to a nap in the interior of his warm box.

If the puppy will not nurse he may be too cold, especially if he is complaining but not doing anything. A good rub with a cloth or a warm-up in the box will usually set him right.

Sometimes a Bullmastiff will have her puppies every half hour, sometimes the intervals are longer. Do not let her go more than about two hours as a delay might indicate a problem and may cause the loss of others waiting in line. If this happens call your vet and discuss it with him or her.

You will have to watch the bitch carefully to tell when she has had her last puppy as Bullmastiffs can have anywhere from four to sixteen. She will normally tell you when she thinks she has finished by settling down for a well-earned sleep. Before she finally settles down, make sure she goes outside and relieves herself. She must do this to ensure her bladder is functioning properly. Most owners need to be a little firm to get the mother to go outside as the last thing she wants to do is leave her brood.

Most whelpings seem to happen at night. If this is the case for your bitch, take her out the following morning and walk her until she evacuates her bowels. Although stimulating milk supply, consumption of the afterbirths also causes constipation. It is advisable not to allow her to eat more than one or two if possible but sometimes it can be difficult to intervene at the appropriate time. She must pass this to allow her bowels to function properly. It will normally appear as a malodorous black, tarry substance, but the sight of it means all is well.

Barbara Shoneck's High Hill's Sugar 'n' Spice with her first litter.

If by chance your bitch has no milk you will have to hand feed the puppies until they are able to feed themselves at about three weeks. In this case check with your breeder what formula you should use, how much and how often. After feeding you will have to play mother and rub the puppy's stomach and genital area with a wet face cloth to imitate the action of a mother's tongue and cause the puppy to relieve itself. Sometimes a milkless bitch will oblige and do the licking for you, but it is better to be prepared. Keep a daily check on the puppies' weights as a guide to see if they are getting enough food.

Problems during whelping

Most whelpings go very easily but now and again there are certain warning signs that things are not going quite as they should. It is best to be ready for these moments so you are not taken unawares.

Straining: If your bitch has been straining and having muscle contractions for about two hours and nothing is happening, the chances are that she is in trouble. There could be many reasons why she cannot deliver.

If you feel she is in this situation call your vet and discuss the possibility with him. He will not perform a caesarian unless it is necessary, so do not feel he will do it for the sake of it. However, if he advises you to take your bitch to his surgery, do so quickly; every minute lost may mean the loss of a puppy. Most bitches, although feeling unhappy with life at this point, are surprisingly docile when asked to accompany you to the veterinary surgery. It is almost as if they know help is there. Keep your bitch warm with a blanket and take a box with a hot water bottle and a towel or two to bring the puppies home in.

Should a Caesarean section be necessary your vet will attend to it immediately. If you have pre-warned him of your litter he may have assistants waiting for his call. If you take him unawares you may have to help by taking the puppies from him as they are born. You now have to play mum completely; the real one is fast asleep on the operating table. Remember about removing the membrane, remember the rubbing to simulate the licking, and do not forget the centrifugal swing. Once you have the pup crying and breathing well, place it in the warm box and await the next one. Sometimes during a caesarian the puppies arrive quickly so you may have to do what is necessary and go back to the box later to complete certain items.

One thing to remember is that your bitch went to sleep with an unpleasant pain in her stomach and will wake up to a box full of crying puppies. It is enough to make any mother want to leave home and certainly enough to make her wonder what is in the box and maybe make her a little strange towards its contents. Understanding and gentleness will be necessary to get your bitch to accept this box full of bobbing heads as her family. Sometimes the affinity is immediate. Often it is not. If she is uncertain or growls you may have to take steps to remedy the situation. Sometimes all that is needed is a good sleep and afterwards everything is fine right down to feeding time. Be patient, but be firm; if she does not take to her litter guess who is going to be playing mother every two hours for the next three weeks!

Growling: A breeder never quite knows how well his bitch will take to puppies for the first time. It is a sad fact, but true, that many of the Bull breeds never like their puppies. In some cases it can be fatal. The mother's reaction is usually very fast so the breeder must be alert and quick to respond if necessary. This does not mean you have to be a poised, nervous wreck, making your bitch edgy, but be prepared. Even though the puppy may have been born naturally and the bitch will have assisted with enthusiasm and dedication, sometimes she will take one look at the newborn and assume an aggressive posture and growl at it. Listen to her and believe her. Sometimes it is nothing more than a scared reaction to motherhood and the uncertainty of what is going on. Usually if the bitch is going to attack the puppy she will not do it until the puppy lifts its head in search of its mother. The growling bitch will interpret this as a challenge stance and strike. It is not pretty, it is not pleasant, and it is always fatal for the puppy. Depending on your bitch, a kind or sharp word

Ch Leathernek's Gift of Gab, CGC, TDI, a first time mother. Note the safety rail around the edge. Owned by Randy and Angie Reese (Ranah).

may be all that is needed to overcome her frightened attitudes. However, if she means business you will have to be on your guard to ensure that you can intercept the new puppy before she has a chance to show her disdain for it.

If she takes this attitude you may have to muzzle her or hold her head down while the puppies nurse, taking them away afterwards. Some bitches will do this and even clean them afterwards, providing they do not come face to face with them. If this relationship can be maintained it is much easier to put up with for three weeks than to have to make formula. Unfortunately, the adrenaline from the aggression is usually enough to remove the natural oxytocin from the blood and halt all production of milk. These two usually go hand in hand and an aggressive bitch has no milk. It is obvious in this situation that the sooner the puppies leave the environment of such a dog and are weaned the better.

Shaking: Sometimes after a bitch has spent a long time whelping, or has given birth to a large litter, she shakes. The shaking resembles someone who has a bad cold and whose muscles are quivering. This is exactly what is happening: the muscles have lost so much calcium that the bitch is suffering from eclampsia, or milk fever. This situation can become serious very quickly, so do not hesitate to call your vet, who will give her a calcium injection. If the shaking is bad, or your vet has a long way to come, give a spoonful of calcium glutonate, available from your chemist. This is only an interim measure as the glutonate does not contain the necessary phosphorous so do not consider it an alternative to an injection.

Hand feeding: If your bitch has no milk, or sometimes after a caesarian section, you may have to help out with the feeding. Advances are always being made in the area of milk substitute and the best guide is to ask your breeder who has probably gone through this a dozen times. On average a puppy will need to be fed about every two hours in the first week. The formula will be accepted best at about body temperature but, like human babies, individual puppies have their preferences. For the first week, the nipples on the bottles will need to be very soft like those used on bottles for premature human babies. Puppies do not suck as such, but create pressure movements at the back of their throats with their jaws. It is when these jaw muscles tire, not how full his stomach is, that tells a new born puppy when to stop sucking. For this reason, in the first few days of hand feeding a puppy whose stomach is full will scream and cry as if he is starving if the actual suckling time has been short. His jaws are not tired, and neither is he, so he feels cheated of food. It is only after about a week that the fullness of the stomach tells the pup when he has had enough. This explains why new puppies seem to lie there forever sucking away when the milk has long gone whether they have managed to get enough or not.

If your puppies seem to be sucking and yet getting no food, a quick before-and-after comparison on the scales will tell you whether you need to tube feed your litter. This is a delicate operation if you are not used to it so enquire about it from your vet beforehand just in case you need it.

If you are playing mother you must remember to stop feeding intermittently, as you would with a human baby, and remove the air from the digestive tract. To do this with a puppy take a wet face cloth and rub the stomach and genital area. The puppy will burp, urinate, and defecate. This may not be pleasant to you but it is necessary. If you attempt further feeding without doing this you will have a wriggly uncomfortable puppy that will cry and complain.

If you do have to play mother, signs to watch for are:

- eyes open at 9 to 12 days
- up and walking by 17 days
- ears open at 17 to 21 days

Puppies lie twitching and 'walking' in their sleep. This is nature's way of trying out the parts, and a perfectly normal, healthy sign of active muscular puppies. Conversely, if a puppy just lies there and sleeps, motionless, bring it to your vet's attention. If you intend to remove any dew claws, these must be surgically removed by the time the puppies are three days old. All nails must be kept short, especially if you intend to show any of the puppies. Prior to serious nail cutting, the little hooks on their nails should be removed carefully with human nail clippers to prevent the puppies from shredding the poor bitch's stomach, and tangling themselves up in any material.

Weaning to Eight Weeks

When the puppies reach the age of three weeks, the bitch will start to object to their new teeth. Up until this time she will have taken care of all toilet cleaning, licking it up as if it were ambrosia. Remember that when weaning time comes you have to be mother, so save large quantities of newspaper and prepare for cleaning up chores.

At about the age of three weeks you will notice a decided lack of enthusiasm on the part of the bitch to stay with her pups for any length of time because of their teeth. Bullmastiff puppies seem to grow teeth like vampires once they start. The puppies may want milk but the last thing the bitch wants is to have a bunch of very active puppies leaping at her and grabbing a mouthful of nipple with sharp teeth. Besides the discomfort, the constant grabbing can damage her mammaries and cause bleeding, infection and permanent damage.

To avoid this, you should watch carefully for the first signs so you can start the weaning process. Puppies will always prefer to lie there sucking effortlessly than to have to work for their food by competing for it or exerting any effort. At 17–21 days the puppies should begin trying to get up and run about. Occasionally there will be a lazy pup who prefers to lie there like a blimp, especially if the mother is a good nurser. Another reason for inactivity is that the puppies' feet might be slipping on the floor. If a puppy has tried repeatedly to stand up and run only to slip back into place, he will lie there and nurse without any further attempt. The problem with this attitude is the puppy's weight is increasing; if it increases while the puppy remains in the lying position the front legs are pushed wider and wider apart. Eventually this 'swimmer' is too heavy for the weak muscles to lift him up and this becomes a permanent feature. Therefore, make sure a non-slip surface is provided. If the puppy still proves to be lazy, remove the bitch

Weaning can be a pleasant, but messy, activity.

from the whelping box for a long enough time to make the puppy very hungry. It is amazing to see an apparently helpless puppy struggle up and walk when mother is close by and the pup is hungry. This kind of puppy must obviously be trimmed down in weight and a little hunger will soon attend to the matter.

A puppy will ignore a bowl of softened food for the readily-available milk supply lying close by. The secret to weaning is competition. Take the puppy food of choice and dilute it to make a sloppy, watery mixture. It is wise to dilute the puppy version of the dog food you intend to use when the puppies get old enough for solid food. Do not add sundry items to this mixture as you will only cause stomach upsets. Do not use any cow's milk. The lacto bacillus bacteria in the puppy is the same as that in the bitch's milk, so if you introduce another you have a likely candidate for diarrhoea. If your puppy has a digestive problem, the naturally homogenised milk from a female goat is easily digestible and readily acceptable.

After the last feed take your bitch away and let her enjoy her day well away from the pups. When feeding time comes again the puppies will start to complain and you must be sure to prevent the bitch's natural instinct to answer this call. When another half hour has gone by, introduce your puppy bowl with your mixture. Hunger will drive the puppies to investigate a possible source of nourishment and most take quite naturally to lapping, sucking, or slipping their way through the gooey mix. Most end up wearing some of it.

When they have had enough, and this is quite soon the first time, let the mother go into the whelping box. She will be greeted by shrieks of welcome from the pups, but when they come to nurse they quickly find their appetite has diminished. Mother will do a nice clean-up of heads and tails and the puppies will sleep well that night with a good solid meal in their stomachs. Start weaning feeds at four-hour intervals and adjust this as the meals get heavier.

The mixture can become more solid at each subsequent mealtime. If at one meal it seems a little too much work for the puppies, return to yesterday's mix and try again tomorrow. The reduction in suckling will help the bitch's milk supply to dry up gradually. Once the pups are eating well in this manner the bitch can be moved to her own quarters to allow her peace and quiet.

There is an age-old remedy for drying up the bitch's milk after weaning which still works well. For about three or four days, reduce the bitch's water intake (but not enough to cause dehydration). Smooth camphor oil onto the mammaries in the morning and vinegar in the evening, and you will

Remember to keep the puppies' nails short, especially if they are still feeding from the bitch.

Bess, foster mum to ...

...two bitches who both became champions.

find the bitch regains her girlish figure very quickly without the characteristic droop associated with matrons. Do not rub these mixtures onto her, as the rubbing will stimulate milk production. Once you have started this procedure, do not allow the puppies to nurse as the camphor is harmful to them.

Your bitch may have been a good mother, but very likely wants her own space back as soon as her puppies have left home. Therefore she may not enjoy the company of any of her pups after weaning. The Bullmastiff owner will have to watch for this and take care that the bitch's natural territorial attitudes do not create problems in the household. A word of caution to novice breeders: take care if you reintroduce puppies to the bitch after a separation. Some mothers are loving and only too pleased to see their young. However, many have no time for this reunion, having resumed their prior role as protector and territorial patrol dog. If this is the case the bitch may not welcome the intrusion of 'strange' dogs on her ground, even if they are her young. Such territorial behaviour must be carefully watched to avoid any trouble. If the bitch shows an obvious antipathy, take the puppies well away; do not risk trouble. It is a wonderful sight to see a bitch playing with her weaned young, but the converse is not so good.

Different cultures have varied ideas but most agree that the best time to worm puppies is at three, six and nine weeks of age. It makes no sense to feed good food to nematodes when it could be benefiting the puppies. The chances of the puppies carrying worms through hormone migration from the bitch is about 99% so initial wormings do not normally require proof through stool samples. Modern worm medications are well balanced to allow puppy worming without worry.

Before this time has arrived you should have had a discussion with your vet concerning vaccination of the litter. The vaccination will again depend on the situation relating to the most feared diseases of distemper, hepatitis, leptospirosis, parvovirus, and corona. These are not words meant to scare you, but real potential epidemics if you do not attend to them. Most breeders and vets agree that these vaccinations must all be taken care of by no later than eight weeks. Further vaccinations will be advised at this time by your vet. In countries where rabies is a problem a vaccination will be given after the puppies are three months old.

EIGHT

CHAPTER EIGHT

Bullmastiff Breed Standards

Am Ch Ladybug I'm Rose Barrette. Winner of the 1993 Canadian National Specialty.

1. Muzzle
2. Occiput
3. Stop
4. Cheek
5. Flew
6. Arch of neck
7. Withers
8. Loin
9. Hock
10. Pastern
11. Toes
12. Point of elbow
13. Forearm (humerus)
14. Brisket
15. Shoulder
16. Ribs
17. Flank
18. First thigh
19. Stifle
20. Second thigh
21. Tail

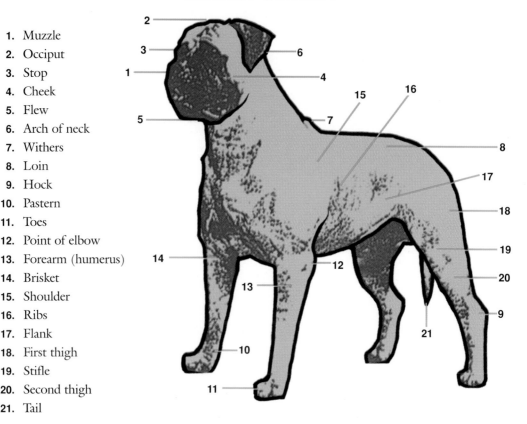

The parts of the Bullmastiff.

What is a Standard?

All pure-bred dogs started out as cross-breeds from whatever strains were indigenous to them, evolving in accordance with local circumstances. Eventually the people would rely on the dogs to do certain jobs for them and fulfil a particular criterion. In some cases it was guarding the flocks; in some, herding sheep; in others a tracking nose, or the ability to go to ground after vermin, led to the dogs being used for these purposes.

All the early dogs were used for one or more specific functions, as they could not be kept for amusement or play; they had to earn their living. Ultimately the dog owners would agree on what was needed to satisfy their requirements for a dog to do some specific job. In most cases the choices of type were entirely dependent on function, with no aesthetic considerations whatsoever. Even the white coat of the Sealyham terrier was a functional one so that Captain Edwards, the breed originator, would not mistake his dog for a fox and shoot it by mistake. Once the physical type had been agreed the owners of the breed worked together to perfect the functional and physical characteristics of their dogs. When kennel clubs appeared on the scene it was to these 'fanciers' of common intent and agreement that the kennel clubs looked for guidance in determining the standards needed for the breed in question. To this day, breed standards are determined in the same way.

The autonomous kennel club of every country has the right to re-determine the criteria for any breed. This would happen, for instance, if the standard set down by the breed's country of origin did not use the same terminology as that current in the country of adoption, and ignored local factors governing the development of the breed. Many countries prefer to use the standard of the country of origin as a guide, modifying it later as the breed interest intensifies.

The Bullmastiff Standard

In the following text are the Bullmastiff Standards of the United Kingdom, the United States of America, Canada, South Africa, Australia and New Zealand.

Many hours can be spent discussing each country's development of the breed since its acceptance in Great Britain by the Kennel Club in 1924. In all too many countries where similar dogs have been separated by time and distance a parochial development has evolved based on local ideas and nationalistic pride, formulating a separate breed.

One of the amazing things is the continuity that has followed the Bullmastiff in most of its adoptive countries. To simplify the explanation, understand that Britain, the originator of the breed, recently revised its Standard very slightly from one that had been in use for many, many years. Upon examination it will be seen that Australia's Standard is a virtual carbon copy of the revised standard, while New Zealand's is a carbon copy of the original British Standard.

South Africa uses the original British Standard as its base with a few changes in terminology but not in meaning, probably for easier regional understanding. An admirable addition to the end of the South African Standard is the space given to comments on personality traits, the adult dog, and temperament. This is a far-sighted addition which can only assist novice owners and should be considered by other countries.

Although the thought of an International Standard on Bullmastiffs creates logistical nightmares, it is interesting that the commonwealth countries mentioned are attempting just that within their jurisdictions. This approach at least attempts to bring the type into common line and allows the avenues of modern communication to remove physical distance barriers.

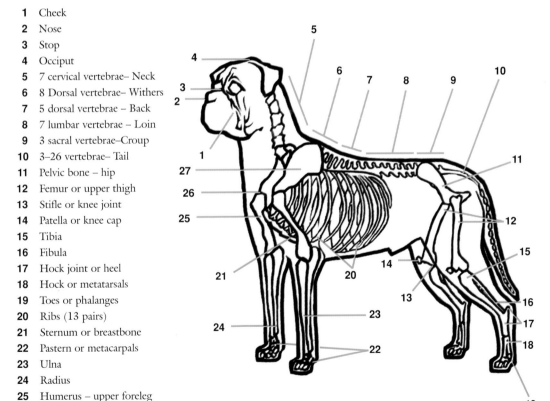

1   Cheek
2   Nose
3   Stop
4   Occiput
5   7 cervical vertebrae– Neck
6   8 Dorsal vertebrae– Withers
7   5 dorsal vertebrae – Back
8   7 lumbar vertebrae – Loin
9   3 sacral vertebrae–Croup
10 3–26 vertebrae– Tail
11 Pelvic bone – hip
12 Femur or upper thigh
13 Stifle or knee joint
14 Patella or knee cap
15 Tibia
16 Fibula
17 Hock joint or heel
18 Hock or metatarsals
19 Toes or phalanges
20 Ribs (13 pairs)
21 Sternum or breastbone
22 Pastern or metacarpals
23 Ulna
24 Radius
25 Humerus – upper foreleg
26 Shoulder joint
27 Scapula or shoulder blade

Anatomy of the Bullmastiff.

99

Back left: Ch Nightbeauty Benson Lee. Back centre: Nightbeauty Tudor Cassie. Back right: Ch Nightwatch Lady Nikita. Front left: Ch Bulwaren Earl Oplenty. Front right: Bullmaster Lord Darcy. Photograph courtesy of Bullmaster Kennels.

Another member of the commonwealth, Canada, seems to have taken the task of type control one step further. Canada is a country of merging ethnic backgrounds, many of them non-commonwealth, who may not know or care about Bullmastiffs. Perhaps this is why the Canadian Standard has gone to great lengths to ensure a future understanding of the Bullmastiff Standard by extraneous specific descriptions. For whatever reason, the Canadian Standard is so specific that no one can claim to have a hard time interpreting it.

The American Standard has recently been revised and is shown here in its new format. The descriptions are more precise than before, and the sequence of format has been changed to produce a far more understandable breed standard than was previously used. Many of the American breeders are concerned that the Bullmastiff may suffer the same consequence as the Bull Terrier breed and end up as a separate American breed. Although this is the prerogative of the American Bullmastiff Fancier there are many who would prefer to see it stay as the dog that first impressed them and attracted them to the breed. To this extent, many American breeders have taken to importing British dogs to retain the British influence in their lines. Only the American Bullmastiff fanciers will ultimately decide what will happen. Although the commonwealth standard may extend with more specifics than necessary to the Canadian/American border, the Bullmastiff may be at the junction of a new era in American history.

British exhibitor/breeder and breed judge Mr H J Price makes the following comments on the Breed Standard:

In my opinion the standard for any breed of dog should be that of its country of origin. What use is there in importing a dog and then changing its looks or type? To me this seems a pointless exercise.

Basically there is no difference between any of the standards. Therefore we have a universally accepted Bullmastiff that can be exhibited and win in any country, which is as it should be.

Our standard has stood for many years with only minor additions or alterations. It is not complicated, but easily understood by all. That it has stood for so long is a tribute to those who wrote the original standard. Over the years there have been those who sought to make changes; mostly I would suggest those who wanted to make the standard fit their dogs and always those who had very little knowledge of the breed.

The Bullmastiff is now recognised world-wide. I would not suggest that everyone follows our standard; far from it! But I would say let us keep at least a similar basically acceptable standard.

As a show judge, I totally agree with Mr Price on this, and it should be applied to all breeds.

Why Is a Bullmastiff the Way He Is?

The criteria for the Bullmastiff did not happen by accident. There was definite reasoning behind the decisions of the early gamekeepers to 'design' the Bullmastiff the way he was. The gamekeeper was using an animal against men who had nothing to lose but their lives and everything to gain by fighting back. The gamekeepers had to produce a dog that could withstand any and all abuse that these desperate, intelligent poachers could produce and all the dog had to defend himself with was his 'natural' physical body. Some of the points are obvious, others more subtle.

Head and skull

The skull is built like a square fortified box that allows for much punishment without the loss of all senses. If the dog is damaged on one side of the head the wideness and squareness allows for the dog still to function with the other side. A narrow or snipey skull could easily be crushed by a foot or club but the wide broad skull prevents this. The eyes at each side of the wide head act as the same safeguard. If one eye is damaged the other side of the head can still work and if the dog is hit squarely across the face the flatness can take the blow whereas a Borzoi-type dog would be killed.

The muzzle performs in parallel to the head. The wideness and 'chopped-off' appearance assures minimum damage and allows the dog the greatest leverage if he has to grab the intruder's club or stick. The wide-spaced canines and flat-fronted muzzle permit the dog to hold very tightly with his strong cheek muscles and yet continue to breathe. The abbreviation of flews ensures a relatively dry mouth that will not slide or slip while the dog is gripping.

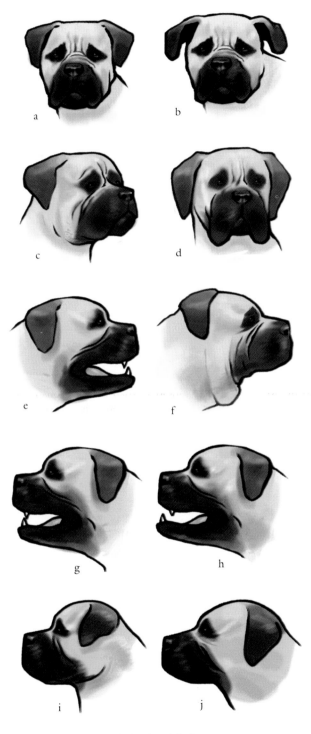

The head and skull.
(a) Good ear set. (b) Poor ear set. (c) Good flews.
(d) Flews too pendulous. (e) Good bite. (f) Throaty.
(g) Good bite. (h) Poor bite (undershot). (i) Good stop.
(j) Poor stop and snipey.

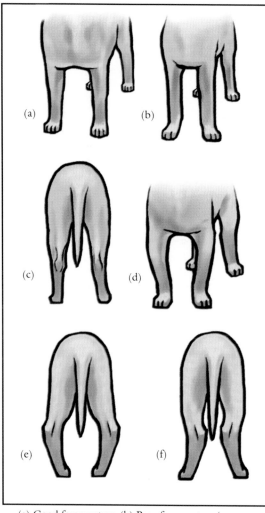

(a) Good forequarters. (b) Poor forequarters (narrow front). (c) Good hindquarters. (d) Out at elbow. (e) Sickle hocked. (f) Cow hocked.

The ears are small to prevent the poacher or intruder from gaining an advantage by grabbing the dog's ears and using the hand hold as a means to free himself from the dog.

Light eyes have always been a fault in this breed. If you are lying in wait for an intruder the last thing you need is for him to see the moon reflecting off your dog's eyes. The dark eyes form an integral part of the mask effect to break up the outline of the dog's face in the dark. Light eyes would show up well against the dark marking that surrounds Bullmastiff's eyes.

Forequarters

A Bullmastiff is not a dog that pursues its prey and jumps on it as a German Shepherd might. The Bullmastiff is a 'knock down and pin' dog. To do the knocking down the Bullmastiff uses its huge chest of great width and depth as a bulldozer would use its blade. To achieve this the Bullmastiff needs its chest and the accompanying wide stance and shoulder muscles. The correct proportion of his upper and lower front legs give the proper leverage and balance as the dog hits the intruder.

Back and hindquarters

The forequarters and hindquarters work together as one. The hind end supplies the power to move the dog from his lying position to an immediate charging mode, delivering power and speed to the business front end to knock down the adversary. All this is delivered through the connecting transmission of the dog's back. To coordinate the front and rear into an efficient working team the dog needs a powerful short back that will not suffer from weakness of length or rigidity of shortness, giving the dog the ability to twist and turn. Hindquarters should have well-developed second thighs to allow quick action from a lying position.

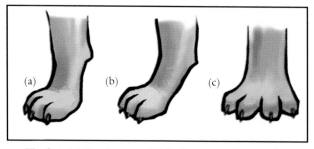

The feet. (a) Good pastern. (b) Slack pastern. (c) Splay foot.

Feet

The feet are described as arched, well-muscled, cat-like. The dog was not operating in wide open spaces, but rather in and out of thickets and trees. To do this well the dog needed strong feet that could pivot his weight and bulk around trees and up rock faces; in the most adverse surface areas, he also needed strong, hard pads.

Tail

Many people think of a tail as an unnecessary extra piece at the back end of the dog. The Bullmastiff needed his tail as a counterbalance as he did his twisting and turning. A dog's body works like a cantilever bridge and must always be kept in balance. The work of a Bullmastiff emphasises this perfectly.

Coat

In his original role, the Bullmastiff must have spent many wet and uncomfortable hours lying in the grass waiting for his quarry. It is obvious that he would need a weatherproof coat to do this job; otherwise he would not have lasted long. Originally, gamekeepers favoured brindle for their dogs. A good brindle has a base colour (usually of fawn or red) with vertical tiger striping. Quite often today unknowing fanciers will refer to any dark colouring on a lighter background as brindle, but this is not true. The striping of a brindle was as valuable to the early gamekeeper and his night dog as stripes are for a zebra's survival on the savanna of Africa. The Bullmastiff had to blend in with the background to give him and his master every advantage.

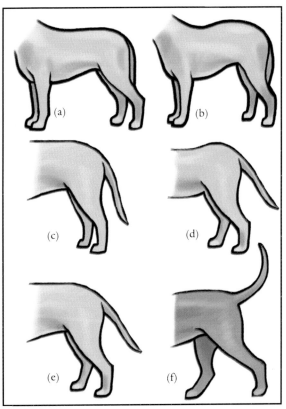

(a) Well balanced. (b) Roach backed. (c) Straight stifle.
(d) Sway backed. (e) Good tail carriage.
(f) Hound or gay tail.

The Standard in the United Kingdom

General appearance: Powerful build, symmetrical, showing great strength, but not cumbersome; sound and active.
Characteristics: Powerful, enduring, active and reliable.
Temperament: High spirited, alert and faithful.
Head and skull: Skull large and square, viewed from every angle, fair wrinkle when interested, but not when in repose. Circumference of skull may equal height of dog measured at top of shoulder; broad and deep with well filled cheeks. Pronounced stop. Muzzle short; distance from tip of nose to stop approximately one third of length from tip of nose to centre of occiput, broad under eyes and sustaining nearly same width to end of nose; blunt and cut off square, forming right angle with upper line of face, and at same time proportionate with skull. Under-jaw broad to end. Nose broad with widely spreading nostrils; flat, neither pointed nor turned up in profile. Flews not pendulous, never hanging below level of lower jaw.
Eyes: Dark or hazel, of medium size, set apart the width of muzzle with furrow between. Light or yellow eyes highly undesirable.
Ears: V-shaped, folded back, set on wide and high, level of occiput giving square appearance to skull which is most important. Small and deeper in colour than body. Point of ear level with eye when alert. Rose ears highly undesirable.
Mouth: Level desired but slightly undershot allowed but not preferred. Canine teeth large and set wide apart, other teeth strong, even and well placed.

Ch Maggie May of Bunsoro.

Can Am Ch Shayla's Levi Alargh Ddu winning the 1991 Canadian Speciality. Bred by the author, pictured far right.

Neck: Well arched, moderate length, very muscular and almost equal to skull in circumference.

Forequarters: Chest, wide and deep, well let down between forelegs, with deep brisket. Shoulders muscular, sloping and powerful, not overloaded. Forelegs powerful and straight, well boned, set wide apart, presenting a straight front. Pasterns straight and strong.

Body: Back short and straight, giving compact carriage, but not so short as to interfere with activity. Roach and sway backs highly undesirable.

Hindquarters: Loins wide and muscular with fair depth of flank. Hind legs strong and muscular, with well developed second thighs, denoting power and activity, not cumbersome. Hocks moderately bent. Cow hocks highly undesirable.

Feet: Well arched, cat like, with rounded toes, pads hard. Dark toe nails desirable. Splayed feet highly undesirable.

Tail: Set high, strong at root and tapering, reaching hocks, carried straight or curved, but not hound fashion. Crank tails highly undesirable.

Gait/movement: Movement indicates power and sense of purpose. When moving straight neither front nor hind legs should cross or plait, right front and left rear leg rising and falling at same time.

SA Ch Chizelhurst Chimurenga, Best Cape Bullmastiff Dog 1993.

A firm back line unimpaired by powerful thrust from hind legs denoting a balanced and harmonious movement.

Coat: Short and hard, weather resistant, lying flat to body. Long, silky or woolly coats highly undesirable.

Colour: Any shade of brindle, fawn or red; colour to be pure and clear. A slight white marking on chest permissible. Other white markings undesirable. Black muzzle essential, toning off towards eyes, with dark markings around eyes contributing to expression.

Size: Height at shoulder: dogs 63.5–68.5cm (25–27in); bitches 61–66cm (24–26 in). Weight: Dogs 50–59kg (110–130lb); bitches 41–50kg (90–110lb).

Faults: Any departure from the foregoing points should be considered a fault and the seriousness with which the fault should be regarded should be in exact proportion to its degree.

Note: Male animals should have two apparently normal testicles fully descended into the scrotum. Reproduced courtesy of The Kennel Club.

The Standard in South Africa

The Kennel Union of Southern Africa follows the principle that the standard of a breed should follow that of the country of origin. Thus each point mentioned in the previous British standard should also be read as South African.

The Standard in Australia

General appearance: Powerful build, symmetrical, showing great strength, but not cumbersome; sound and active.

Characteristics: Powerful, enduring, active and reliable.

Temperament: High spirited, alert and faithful.

Head and skull: Skull large and square, viewed from every angle; fair wrinkle when interested, but not when in repose. Circumference of skull may equal height of dog measured at top of shoulder; broad and deep with well filled cheeks. Pronounced stop. Muzzle short; distance from tip of nose to stop approximately one third of length from tip of nose to centre of occiput; broad under eyes and sustaining nearly same width to end of nose; blunt and cut off square, forming right angle with upper line of face, and at same time proportionate with skull. Under-jaw broad to end. Nose broad with widely spreading nostrils; flat, neither pointed nor turned up in profile. Flews not pendulous, never hanging below level of lower jaw.

Eyes: Dark or hazel, of medium size, set apart the width of muzzle with furrow between. Light or yellow eyes highly undesirable.

Ch Nightwatch Brahms' Lullaby.

Aust Ch Bullpower Olympia.

Ears: V-shaped, folded back, set on wide and high, level with occiput giving square appearance to skull which is most important. Small and deeper in colour than body. Point of ear level with eye when alert. Rose ears highly undesirable.

Mouth: Level desired but slightly undershot allowed but not preferred. Canine teeth large and set wide apart, other teeth strong, even and well placed.

Neck: Well arched, moderate length, very muscular and almost equal to skull in circumference.

Forequarters: Chest wide and deep, well let down between forelegs, with deep brisket. Shoulders muscular, sloping and powerful, not overloaded. Forelegs powerful and straight, well boned, set wide apart, presenting a straight front. Pasterns straight and strong.

Body: Back short and straight, giving compact carriage, but not so short as to interfere with activity. Roach and sway backs highly undesirable.

Hindquarters: Loins wide and muscular with fair depth of flank. Hind legs strong and muscular, with well developed second thighs, denoting power and activity, not cumbersome. Hocks moderately bent. Cow hocks highly undesirable.

Feet: Well arched, cat-like, with rounded toes, pads hard. Dark toe nails desirable. Splayed feet highly undesirable.

Tail: Set high, strong at root and tapering, reaching to hocks, carried straight or curved, but not hound fashion. Crank tails highly undesirable.

Gait/movement: Movement indicates power and sense of purpose. When moving straight, neither front nor hind legs should cross or plait, right front and left rear leg rising and falling at the same time. A firm back line unimpaired by powerful thrust from hind legs denoting a balanced and harmonious movement.

Coat: Short and hard, weather resistant, lying flat to body. Long, silky or woolly coats highly undesirable.

Colour: Any shade of brindle, fawn or red; colour to be pure and clear. A slight white marking on chest permissible. Other white markings undesirable. Black muzzle essential, toning off towards eyes, with dark markings around eyes contributing to expression.

Size: Height at shoulder: dogs 63.5cm–68.5cm (25–27 in); bitches 61–66cm (24–26in). Weight: dogs 50–59kg (110–130lb); bitches 41–50 kg (90–110lb).

Faults: Any departure from the foregoing points should be considered a fault and the seriousness with which the fault should be regarded should be in exact proportion to its degree.

Note: Male animals should have two apparently normal testicles fully descended into the scrotum.

The Standard in the United States of America

General appearance: That of a symmetrical animal, showing great strength, endurance, and alertness; powerfully built but active. The foundation breeding was 60% Mastiff and 40% Bulldog.

Ch Licassa Delightful Lady of Oldwell aged 9 months.

Am & Ber Ch Ladybug Thorn of the Rose.

Am Can Ch Windridge Absolute Reality TT.

Multiple Ch Dox Fast Freddy of Shady Oak.

The breed was developed in England by gamekeepers for protection against poachers.

Size, proportion, substance: *Size* – Dogs, 25 to 27 inches at the withers, and 110 to 130 pounds weight. Bitches, 24 to 26 inches at the withers, and 100 to 120 pounds weight. Other things being equal, the more substantial dog within these limits is favoured. *Proportion* – The length from tip of breastbone to rear of thigh exceeds the height from withers to ground only slightly, resulting in a nearly square appearance.

Head: *Expression* – Keen, alert and intelligent. *Eyes* – Dark and of medium size. *Ears* – V-shaped and carried close to the cheeks, set on wide and high, level with occiput and cheeks, giving a square appearance to the skull; darker in colour than the body and medium in size. *Skull:* Large, with a fair amount of wrinkle when alert; broad, with cheeks well developed. Forehead flat. *Stop* – Moderate. *Muzzle* – Broad and deep; its length, in comparison with that of the

Ch Ladybug Lady Caitlin.

entire head, approximately as 1 is to 3. Lack of fore-face with nostrils set on top of muzzle is a reversion to the Bulldog and is very undesirable. A dark muzzle is preferable. *Nose* – Black, with nostrils large and broad. *Flews* – Not too pendulous. *Bite* – Preferably level or slightly undershot. Canine teeth large and set wide apart.

Neck, Topline, Body: *Neck* – Slightly arched, of moderate length, very muscular, and almost equal in circumference to the skull. *Topline* – Straight and level between withers and loin. *Body* – Compact, chest wide and deep, with ribs well sprung and well set down between the forelegs. *Back* – Short, giving the impression of a well balanced dog. *Loin* – Wide, muscular, and slightly arched, with fair depth of flank. *Tail* – Set on high, strong at the root, and tapering to the hocks. It may be straight or curved, but never carried hound fashion.

Forequarters: Shoulders muscular but not loaded, and slightly sloping. Forelegs straight, well boned, and set well apart; elbows turned neither in nor out. Pasterns straight, feet of medium size, with round toes well arched. Pads thick and tough, nails black.

Hindquarters: Broad and muscular, with well developed second thigh denoting power, but not cumbersome. Moderate angulation at hocks. Cowhocks and splay feet are serious faults.

Coat: Short and dense, giving good weather protection.

Colour: Red, fawn, or brindle. Except for a very small white spot on the chest, white marking is considered a fault.

Gait: Free, smooth, and powerful. When viewed from the side, reach and drive indicate maximum use of the dog's moderate angulation. Back remains level and firm. Coming and going, the dog moves in a straight line. Feet tend to converge under the body, without crossing over, as speed increases. There is no twisting in or out at the joints.

Temperament: Fearless and confident yet docile. The dog combines the reliability, intelligence, and willingness to please required in a dependable family companion and protector.

The Standard in New Zealand

Characteristics: The temperament of the Bullmastiff combines high spirits, reliability, activity, endurance and alertness.

General appearance: The Bullmastiff is a powerfully built, symmetrical dog, showing great strength, but not cumbersome.

Head and skull: The skull should be large and square, viewed from every angle, with fair wrinkle when interested, but not when in repose. The circumference of the skull may equal the height of the dog measured at the top of the shoulder; it should be broad and deep with good cheeks. The muzzle short, the distance from the tip of the nose to the stop should be approximately one-third of the length from the tip of the nose to the centre of the occiput, broad under the eyes and nearly parallel in width to the end of the nose; blunt and cut off square, forming a right angle with the upper line of the face, and at the same time proportionate with the skull. Under jaw broad to the end. Nose broad with widely spreading nostrils when viewed from the front; flat, not pointed or turned up in profile. Flews not pendulous, and not hanging below the level of the bottom of the lower jaw. Stop definite.

Eyes: Dark or hazel, of medium size, set apart the width of the muzzle with furrow between. Light or yellow eyes a fault.

Ears: V-shaped or folded back, set on wide and high, level with occiput, giving a square appearance to the skull, which is important. They should be small and deeper in colour than the body, the point of the ear should be level with the eye when alert. Rose ears penalised.

Ch Guardall Corvair.

Ch Faith of Arapeti.

Mouth: Mouth to be level, slight undershot allowed, but not preferred. Canine teeth large and set wide apart, other teeth strong, even and well placed. Irregularity of teeth a fault.

Neck: Well-arched, moderate length, very muscular and almost equal to the skull in circumference.

Forequarters: Chest, wide and deep, well set down between forelegs, with deep brisket. Shoulders muscular, sloping and powerful, not overloaded. Forelegs powerful and straight, well boned, and set wide apart, presenting a straight front. Pasterns straight and strong.

Body: Back short and straight, giving compact carriage, but not so short as to interfere with activity. Roach and sway backs a fault.

Hindquarters: Loins wide and muscular with fair depth of flank. Hind legs strong and muscular, with well developed second thighs, denoting power and activity, but not cumbersome. Hocks moderately bent. Cow hocks a fault.

Feet: Not large, with rounded toes, well-arched (cat feet), pads hard. Splay feet a fault.

Tail: Set high, strong at root and tapering, reaching to the hocks, carried straight or curved, but not hound fashion. Crank tails a fault.

Coat: Short and hard, giving weather protection, lying flat to the body. A tendency to long, silky or woolly coats to be penalised.

Colour: Any shade of brindle, fawn or red, but the colour is to be pure and clear. A slight white marking on chest permissible but not desirable. Other white markings a fault. A dark muzzle is essential, toning off towards the eyes, with dark markings around the eyes giving expression. Dark toenails desirable.

Weight and size: Dogs should be 25 to 27in at the shoulder, and 110 to 130lb in weight. Bitches should be 24 to 26in at the shoulder and 90 to

110lb in weight. It must be borne in mind that size must be proportionate with weight, and soundness and activity is most essential.

The Standard in Canada

Note: Faults are classified as Serious or Minor, indicated as (S) and (M) respectively. Note that **minor** faults are points which would not of themselves contribute to unsoundness in the dog, or are the result of poor conditioning, which might be controlled, and are not likely to be hereditary.

Origin and purpose: The Bullmastiff was developed in England by gamekeepers for protection against poachers. The foundation breeding of the modern pure-bred was 60% Mastiff and 40% Bulldog. It is a guard and companion dog, and should be loyal, obedient and thus suitable for training.

General appearance: The Bullmastiff is a powerfully built, symmetrical dog, showing great strength and activity, but not cumbersome; upstanding and compact in appearance, with breadth and depth of skull and body, the latter set on strong, sturdy, well boned legs. The height measured vertically from the ground to the highest point of the withers, should nearly equal the length measured horizontally from the forechest to the rear part of the upper thigh, and should slightly exceed the height at the hips. Bitches are feminine in appearance, of somewhat lighter bone structure than the male, but should still convey strength. *Faults:* (S) Lack of balance. Poor or light bone structure. (M) Lack of muscular development. Ranginess.

Temperament: The Bullmastiff should be bold, fearless and courageous, a dependable guard dog; alert and intelligent. *Faults:* (S) Viciousness. Shyness. (Such dogs should not be used for breeding.) (M) Apathy and sluggishness.

Size: Height at the highest point of the withers – dogs, 25–27in; bitches, 24–26in. *Weight:* Dogs, 110–130lb; bitches, 100–120lb. It is important that weight be in proportion to height and bone structure, to ensure balance. *Faults:* (S) Over maximum height. Under minimum height. (M) Over maximum weight. Under minimum weight.

Coat and colour: *(a) Coat:* short and dense, giving good weather protection. *Faults:* (S) Long, soft coat.(M) 'Staring' coat, which means poor

Centre: Can Ch Shayla's Meet In Montana. Left: Montana's Home To Shylo. Right: Montana's Sunshine Susie Q.

condition. *(b) Colour:* Any shade of red, fawn or brindle, but the colour to be pure and clear. A small white marking on chest permissible but not desirable. *Faults:* (S) White markings other than on chest. (M) Black shading on body, legs or tail (of reds or fawns).

Head: *(a) Skull:* The skull should be large, equal in breadth, length and depth, with a fair amount of wrinkle when the dog is interested; well developed cheeks. The skull in circumference may measure the height of the dog. Forehead flat, with furrow between the eyes. Stop definite. *Faults:* (S) Narrow skull. Shallow skull. (M) Domed forehead. Insufficient stop. *(b) Muzzle:* The muzzle should be short, broad and deep, in the same proportion as the skull. The distance from the tip of the nose to the stop should not exceed one-third of the length from the tip of the nose to the centre of the occiput. Broad under the eyes and nearly parallel in width to the end of the nose; blunt and cut off square, appearing in profile in a plane parallel to the line of the skull. A black mask is essential. The nose should be black; flat; broad with widely spreading nostrils when viewed from the front. Flews not too pendulous. The lower jaw broad. *Faults:* (S) Muzzle too long, too narrow, pointed or lacking in depth. Muzzle too short; nostrils set on top; nose pointed, upturned or laid back; lower jaw narrow. (M) Lack of wrinkle; flews too pendulous. *Disqualifications:* Liver mask. No Mask. *(c) Teeth:* Preferably level bite or slightly undershot. Canine teeth large and set wide apart; other teeth strong, even and well placed. *Faults:* (S) Teeth overshot. Teeth more than 0.25in undershot. Wry mouth. (M) Irregular or poorly placed teeth. Small teeth. *(d) Eyes:* Dark or hazel, and of medium size; set apart the width of the muzzle. *Faults:* (M) Light eyes. Eyes too close

Can Ch Shayla's Promised Rose.

together, too large, too small. *Disqualifications:* Yellow eyes. *(e) Ears:* V-shaped and carried close to the cheeks; set on wide and high, level with the occiput, giving a square appearance to the skull which is important. They should be darker in colour than the body, and the point of the ear, when alert, should be level with the eye. *Faults:* (S) Rose ears. (M) Ears too long or too short. Lack of darker colour.

Neck: Well arched, of moderate length, very muscular, and almost equal in circumference to the skull. *Faults:* (S) Neck too short; too long. Neck weak and scrawny.

Forequarters: Proper angulation and proportionate bone lengths of the forequarters are very important. The shoulder bone should slope forward and downward from the withers at an angle of 45 degrees from the vertical. The humerus (upper arm) should form a right angle with the shoulder bone, 45 degrees from the vertical. The shoulder bone and humerus should be approximately equal in length. The length of the foreleg from the ground to the elbow should be a little more than half the distance from the ground to the withers, approximately 52%. The shoulders and upper arms should be muscular and powerful, but not overloaded. Forelegs powerful, with round heavy bone, vertical and parallel to each other, set well apart; elbows set close to the body. Pasterns straight and strong. Feet of medium size, not turning in or out, with round toes, well arched. Pads thick and tough. Nails black. *Faults:* (S) Lack of proportion in bone. Shoulders too steep. Shoulders overloaded. Elbows turned in or out. Lack of bone in forelegs. Forelegs bowed. Weak pasterns. Splay feet. (M) Feet turned in or out. White nails.

Body and tail: *(a) Body:* Compact. Chest wide and deep, with ribs well sprung and well set down between the forelegs. Back short and level. Loins wide, muscular; croup slightly arched, with fair depth of flank. *Faults:* (S) Body too long. Shallow chest. Narrow chest. Lack of rib-spring. Sway back. Roach back. Tip of hip bone higher than withers. (M) Too much tuck-up. *(b) Tail:* Set on high, strong at the root and tapering to the hocks. It may be carried straight or curved. *Faults:* (S) Screw tail. Crank tail. Tail set too low. (M) Tail carried hound fashion. Too Long. Too short. Too heavily coated.

Hindquarters: It is important that structure, angulation and proportionate bone lengths of the hindquarters be in balance with the forequarters. The pelvis (hip bone) should slope backward and downward from the spine at an angle of 30 degrees. The femur (upper thigh bone) should form a right angle with the pelvis. The lower thigh bone (stifle) should set an angle of 45 degrees to the vertical. The pelvis and femur should be approximately equal in length. The ratio of the lengths of the femur to the tibia-fibula, to the hock should be approximately as 4:5:3. The length of the lower leg, from the ground to the hock joint, should be a little less than 30% of the distance from the ground to the top of the hip bones. The lower leg should be vertical to the ground. The hips should be broad, in balance with shoulders and rib cage. Hind legs strong and muscular, with well developed second thighs, denoting power and activity, but not cumbersome, set parallel to each other and well apart, in balance with forelegs and body. Feet as in forequarters. *Faults:* (S) Lack of proportion in bone. Poor angulation at hip-bone. Narrow hip structure. Stifle too straight or over-angulated. Cow hocks. Bowed hind legs. Splay feet. (M) Feet turned in or out. White nails.

Gait: The gait should be free, balanced and vigorous. When viewed from the side the dog should have good reach in the forequarters and good driving power in the hindquarters. The back should be level and firm, indicating good transmission from rear to front. When viewed from the front (coming toward) or from the rear (going away), at a moderate pace, the dog shall track in two parallel lines, neither too close together nor too far apart, so placed as to give a strong well-balanced movement. The toes (fore and hind) should point straight ahead.

Direction to exhibitors and judges: The dog should be moved in the ring at a sufficient speed to show fluidity of movement, and not at a slow walk. *Faults:* (S) Rolling, paddling, or weaving when gaited. Any crossing movement, either front or rear. Stilted and restricted movement. (Dogs with structural weakness as evidenced by poor movement should not be used for breeding.)

Disqualifications: Liver mask. No mask. Yellow eyes.

CHAPTER NINE

The Problem Times

Bullmaster Sweet Melody (18 mths).
Photo by Animal Pics.

Flying Ears

Like all young animals, your puppy will have a certain amount of stress when he starts to teethe. One of the many ways he shows this is by drooling like a human baby. It is an unpleasant time for your young puppy; his baby teeth are falling out, his mouth is tender, and anything he bites to take away this feeling makes the pain worse. This is the time when your puppy's mature teeth are erupting and, judging by the size of the incoming teeth, it is anything but a pleasant experience.

Depending on the pedigree line, most teething is over by the fourth month, although it does sometimes carry on a little further. One of the tell-tale signs of teething problems is the development of your puppy's ears.

During the time of actual teething, the stress causes the puppy to 'rose' his ears. This is when the ears are pulled back against the side of the head. In extreme cases the burr of the ear is seen.

In most cases the ears return to their natural position against the cheek once teething is over. However, if the teething is particularly bad or the dog has small ears they may have pulled back so far that the muscles do not return the ears to their normal position.

At about five months the cartilage in the ears starts to harden. This means that if your puppy's ears are still rosed at this time they will stay in that position permanently. If the ears show no sign of settling down at about four-and-a-half months it is wise to consider taping them with heating

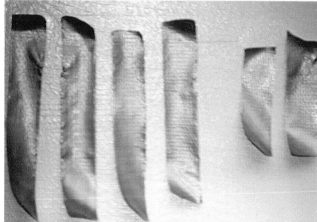

Above left: if the ear cartilage is allowed to harden in this position, the ear set will be spoiled.
Above right: the four long and two short pieces of duct tape needed for ear correction.

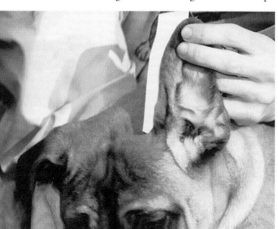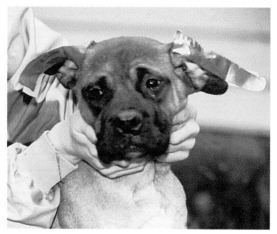

Above left: laying the single piece of tape on the outer edge of the ear leather.
Above right: both ears taped with tab ends hanging prior to pulling ears in line.

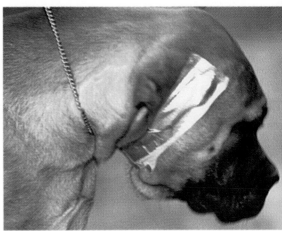

Above: ears pulled in tightly to head by joining the tabs under the chin. Ears seem to be pulled too tightly but this is necessary because of the elasticity of the area.

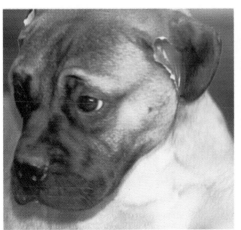

Above: the joining neck tab showing alignment of tape and ear edges pulled in straight line.

duct tape. This is a simple remedy to bring your dog's ears back to normal, and it is completely painless, harmless and takes only a few days. Sounds simple and cheap? It is.

Take two pieces of heating duct tape about 15cm (6in) long and tear them both lengthwise down the middle, making four pieces in all. Next take another piece of duct tape about 8cm (3in) and tear it lengthwise down the middle as well, making two pieces. You should now have six pieces of tape, four 15cm pieces, and two 8cm pieces.

Ask someone to hold the head of the dog while you put the tape in place. Pull one of the ears out straight from the head

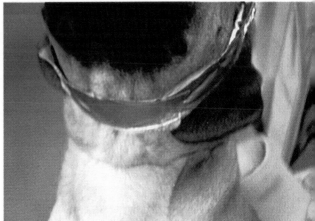

The finished product. Compare this with the first photograph on page 121.

and lay the first long piece on the inside of the top of the leather of the ear from the head outward. If the pieces are torn to the correct length there should be an excess of tape over the end of the ear by about 5cm (2in); this will form a tab. Next, lay another of the long pieces on the outside of the same ear leather in the same way as the first so that the two sticky edges of the tape connect on the top side of the ear leather at the tab end. Repeat the same procedure with the other ear and you will end up with a puppy who looks as if he has a strap hanging from each ear. It is important that the pieces of tape for each ear are put on in two steps. Do not try to put one piece on and fold it over. Although this may seem the smarter move, if you do this you risk rolling the leading edge of the ear, which you will not realise until you take the tapes off. At that stage if you have rolled the edge you may not be able to reverse the situation.

When you have the two tabs in place pull the end of each tab under the chin of the dog quite tightly and use one of the 8cm (3in) pieces of tape to connect the two tabs. Attach the first piece so that the dry side is against the dog and the sticky side out. Use the second piece to cover the sticky exposed side of the tape under the chin to prevent it sticking to everything the puppy touches.

That is all there is to it. In most cases the connection under the chin can be cut after about three days and the ears will magically stay in place in a beautiful ear set. If the set is not quite right simply leaving the tabs on will create enough weight to pull the ears in place over the next few days. Whatever happens, do not leave the tape on for more than a week. If you do this you risk causing ear infection as the ears are held close to the head for too long and the normal circulation of cooling air around the ears is interrupted.

If you remove the tape completely and the ears are not quite what you want, you can always retape them, but remember: the closer to five months the pup gets, the less chance of correction. When you see your dog as a mature animal with a perfect ear set you will appreciate the day you taped his ears.

Margarine will remove any residual tape glue left on the ear hair easily. Be sure to rinse the area well afterwards to prevent any adverse reaction.

Bloat and Gastric Torsion

This very disturbing condition can arise suddenly in the Bullmastiff, often with frightening rapidity. Statistically it only happens to 13 dogs in 10,000 but it is always sensible to be aware of the symptoms in case it happens to your dog.

What is it?
The syndrome is called gastric dilation-torsion. It is a big name for a bloated stomach that twists. This problem seems to affect the larger, deep-chested dog breeds more frequently than others. Simple dilation or bloating can occur at any age but is more frequently seen in young puppies when they have eaten too much too quickly. Gastric torsion can occur at any age but is seen more in older dogs and in more males than females.

How is it caused?
The torsion is initiated by a downward movement of the stomach which, because of the mechanics of its structure, starts a rotation of the stomach either clockwise or anti-clockwise. The direction is not so important as the fact that the gastric distension of the stomach as it twists compresses important veins and arteries in and around the stomach which are needed to nourish the blood cells and keep the blood clear in that area. As the problem increases the stomach impedes the functioning of the heart and lungs and, indirectly, the kidneys. If the situation is not relieved quickly the blood cells will die and prime organs will be irreparably damaged, resulting in perforation, shock and death. This is not meant to alarm you but to illustrate the importance of recognising the potential fatality of this problem and dealing with it immediately.

Symptoms

The usual signs of this problem are restlessness, salivation, retching with no resulting vomit, and abdominal distension. The distended stomach will feel hard and unresponsive to the touch, rather like a drum skin. Such signs develop about three hours after eating and are quite often associated with exercise after feeding. Most dogs will show an outward attitude of depression but the stress of their condition tends to excite them rather than making them stay quiet. Respiration will be rapid, laboured and shallow, typical of shock, and mucous membranes will often show a prolonged refill time.

The distended, hard stomach and a dog who is excited, frightened and in shock are symptoms very hard to miss even to the uninitiated. This is not a condition to be treated lightly. If you see these symptoms call your vet immediately and don't take no for an answer! If your vet is away at the time go to your nearest emergency animal hospital. You will not get a second chance if it is gastric torsion; better a false alarm than a dead Bullmastiff.

Entropion

One of the things that always calls for comment from the all-knowing is the cause of runny eyes. In many cases it is nothing more than a draught that has caught the dog unawares and has resulted in a local irritation to the cornea of the eye, or the more common conjunctivitis. However, there is one more cause that occurs with more than its share of regularity and is never welcome or expected.

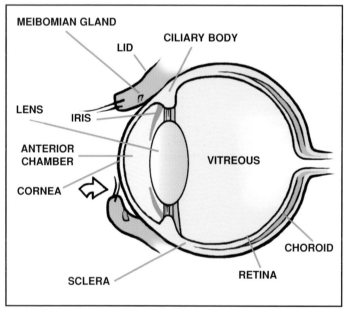

Entropion: the lower lid turns inwards, causing the eyelash to irritate the cornea (arrow indicates the problem).

What is it?

The annoying problem is called entropion. Simply defined, this malady is described as the in-rolling of the eye lid and the accompanying eyelashes.

How is it caused?

It may be an acquired condition where the dog has run into a fence wire or caught his eye on a twig, but unfortunately it is all too often a congenital problem associated with certain pedigree lines.

Symptoms

Sometimes erroneously referred to as 'pink eye', entropion shows itself as discharge from the eye causing obvious irritation and annoyance to the dog. Careful examination will reveal the small hairs and eyelashes rubbing on the bulbous part of the eye. More often than not entropion affects only the lower lid but it can affect the upper as well. Neglect of this condition can lead to damage to the cornea of the eye, prolapse of the iris, and loss of the eye. Often the dog will avoid well-lit places and is seen to blink painfully. The hairs rubbing on the eye creates an ulceration of the eye's surface which often looks red and sore, hence the name of pink-eye.

Depending on the cause of the entropion, the solution may be an easy one. One action that should not be delayed is your call to your vet to determine which kind of entropion your Bullmastiff has and what should be done about it.

Osteochondritis Dissecans (OCD)

It is very normal and quite understandable that a young dog will be full of the joys of spring and want to romp around and jump up and down without a thought or care for what he is doing. One thing that nature does not supply young dogs with is common sense. It may seem fun to chase the cat or young members of the household up and down the stairs, and most people would see nothing wrong with that. But what about jumping down from the back of a truck or a wall? Some people might think this quite normal and acceptable. Think, however, about all that weight coming down on the front legs and shoulders of a young Bullmastiff who still has a large amount of cartilage instead of bone. The mechanical force on the shoulders of, say, an eight-month-old is quite frightening. The result is that something has to give – and it will always be the cartilage, no matter how good the quality of life has been for the young dog.

What is OCD?

In very basic terms, it is a chip of bone cartilage coming off the posterior (back) part of the head of the humerus (upper leg bone of front leg) which gets trapped between the socket joint of the shoulder and the ball of the head of the humerus.

How is it caused?

The head of the humerus is the 'ball' of the ball- and-socket joint of the shoulder (fig 1) which should be smooth and round (fig 2). In osteochondritis dissecans a section of the cartilage and underlying bone becomes partially or completely detached from the head of the humerus (fig 3). The flap of bone can float freely in the joint or may still retain a tenuous attachment to the head of the humerus. The consequence of this loose or detached chip in the joint is inflammation, arthritis and lameness.

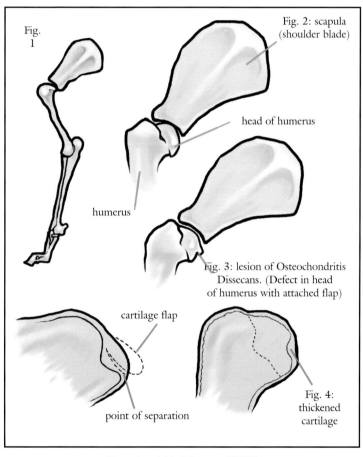

Osteochondritis Dissecans (OCD).

Symptoms

The progression of the symptoms is as follows:

- Foreleg lameness in a young dog with nothing in particular to distinguish this disease from others.
- Although the disease is often present in both legs, lameness of one leg only is usually noticed.
- Signs of lameness may vary in intensity over several weeks or months.
- Pain can sometimes be produced by manipulation of the affected joint.
- In long standing cases, atrophy or wasting of the shoulder muscles may be apparent.
  OCD is probably the most classic of the intensification diseases; due in part to an accelerated

growth rate in which cartilage in the joint becomes abnormally thick, the underlying bone becomes weakened and the joint cartilage collapses into the weakened area of bone creating a chip (fig 4).

Accelerated growth seems to be the major factor in the cause of this disease – either through over-nutrition or genetic selection for large, fast-growing pups. Trauma to the area of weakened cartilage also plays a part, as can be seen by the consistent location of the lesion directly across from the projection at the posterior part of the shoulder blade (see fig 3). In certain postures and gaits this projection on the scapula can impinge strongly on the particular area of the head of the humerus with which we are concerned.

Treatment

The treatment of this disease is, at best, controversial. Most authorities feel that if a large chip is present in the joint, especially if it is still attached, removal by surgery is the treatment of choice.

In mild cases (those with only a small defect in the head of the humerus and no flaps) some researchers suggest strict crate resting for several months and a recheck with X-rays to evaluate the problem area at a later date. If clinical lameness persists and/or the X-ray appearance worsens, surgery may still be performed.

Still other schools of thought have suggested that in some cases rigorous exercise will effect a cure by dislodging the flap from its attachment, causing it to be ground up and allowing the chip(s) to be absorbed and the defect in the humeral head to heal.

As in all such conditions, no consensus has yet been reached on the 'correct' method of treatment. Each vet will have a preference with which he is comfortable.

Hip Dysplasia (HD)

Hip dysplasia is a condition that affects the hip joints of dogs, usually dogs over 13kg (29lb) in weight. The equivalent in those less than 13kg (29lb) is called 'aseptic necrosis of the femoral joints'.

The dysplasia, or sub luxation as it is called by vets, occurs after the femoral head (ball joint) or the cavity (acetabulum) into which it fits in the pelvis has been modified to such an extent that the femoral head no longer fits correctly into the acetabulum, resulting in excessive movement of these two parts. The resultant distress that such movement causes to the joint can be well understood by the layman, as can the pain and arthritic condition that develops. Depending on the condition of the joints when HD is diagnosed, the relative severity can be assessed. In many cases, the pain is so severe and the dog so debilitated that the only kind and humane thing to consider is euthanasia. According to the medical profession, for many, many years HD has been considered a clear case of genetic inferiority of the parents of the dog carrying this dreadful condition.

Here is a theory on hip dysplasia for you to think about; not the normally accepted one, but one that will stimulate thought from the open-minded. Please read the whole story before you pass any judgment; you may be surprised at your deductions after you have read it.

Many years ago, professors of veterinary medicine told us that hip dysplasia was a genetic problem, and that was that. In years gone by the subject of HD was neither current nor a matter of concern to breeders. In the old tradition no fuss was made of the phenomenon and, if a dog showed lameness or strange rear end movement, it was usually put down or at least never used for breeding. It was trial by error. As long as the dog was sound, moved well and showed no trace of exterior problems, no one went looking for trouble. The dogs were used and worked in the true sense of the word and any weakness appeared very quickly as a result of the rigorous life expected of dogs in those days. The occurrences, severity and different types of HD were not considered worthy of study or note.

The breeders of this time had a natural instinct for their stock and knew a good dog by 'feel' and observation. They did not need a pedigree to tell them which was a good specimen; they knew every dog and its offspring for miles around. Long before official standards and recognition, early breeds managed to make it through the ages without X-rays or veterinary intervention. If HD is such a handicap, why was this species of canis not extinct before the dawn of man?

An answer could possibly be staring us in the face. Our social structure and teaching leads us into patterns of behaviour that we accept as unquestionably true and therefore the norm. Take our understanding of HD. Where did you first hear of it? Did you know enough about it to ask questions? Did you really understand where it came from and the deoxyribonucleic acid (DNA) support of it? Do you know the principles of DNA?

What really shook the world of accepted HD data was Cornell University's evidence that HD was not 100% genetic but maybe only 25%, the remainder being environmental. What a shock! However, what did 'environmental' mean? Was that like genetic, only different? Most people accepted the word of Cornell but once again, how many asked, 'Why?' As with much research, principles change by modification every few years, so how accurate are these figures and will they change too? The previous certainty knocked down by this new one makes a breeder pause and wonder...

There is no recorded HD in early British dogs yet it has always been a concern in North America, especially in the heavier breeds. Could it be that different feeding practices in Britain removed or reduced HD? Dogs in Great Britain do tend to be fed on certain items of food which are not used in North America. How many fanciers feed their dogs cows' ears? Or better yet, tripe? The common ingredient in many of these unusual foods is sodium ascorbate, better known as vitamin C. After further thought on this subject a deduction can be made that the high intake of vitamin C has something to do with the collagen in the muscles.

Collagen is the 'glue' that holds muscles together so if there is lots of good glue there are strong muscles, very little or no sub luxation and no acetabuli damage. X-rays are taken to diagnose HD but what

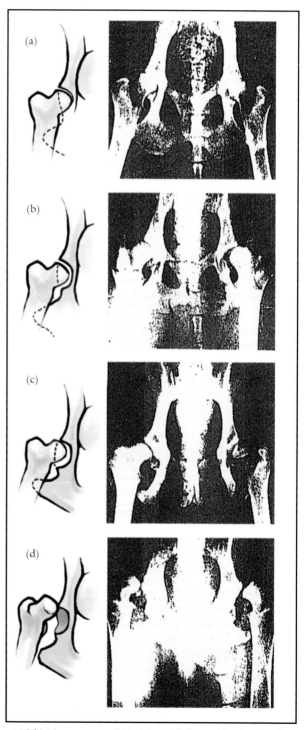

(a) This shows a normal hip joint with femoral head and socket in normal relationship. (b) This shows a 'near normal' joint with head falling away very slightly from the socket. (c) A dysplastic joint – note separation between head and socket. (d) Dysplasia with severe luxation of head out of the socket – note change in shape of both head and socket.

they show us are the results of HD. The bone material and fibre may be fine under normal conditions but, if there is weak musculature that is not holding the ball joint in the acetabulum correctly, the ball joint of the femur will slide and move round until the acetabulum and ball joint are modified sufficiently enough to show up on an X-ray and result in a diagnosis of HD. The apparent physical cause is determined as joint laxity, shallow acetabuli or joint ball head erosion but the observer may be looking at the symptom, not the cause. The use of sodium ascorbate could in itself account for the low rate of HD occurrences in Great Britain. Add to this the slower pace of life in Britain compared to North America and a totally less stressful way of life and a better environment emerges.

For many centuries the Masetheff, or mastiff type of dog, spent most of his day lolling around the manor house, stable or farm with no other concern than where the next meal was coming from. His life was mostly rural, low stress and self-fulfilling. His duties were often learned from an older, trained dog and by sympathetic induction he completed his life's chores. Compare this to today's dog. Higher intensity of social environment, close quarters with other animals, humans by the gross, noise, training, neurotic owners, vaccinations, surgery, showing... Just look at the trauma in a dog's eyes at the first show. The dogs, the noises, the public address system, irritated exhibitors, crowded quarters — a campaign trail where all these problems are compounded, plus the life in a crate which erodes his constitution and muscle tone. These 'evolved' breeds managed to make it through at least 2000 years without any of this but look what's happened in less than 100 years of man's 'concern' for his dog.

Stress is the number one killer in North America, as well as being the prime cause of numerous conditions in animals, and dogs in particular. Stress depletes the vitamin C in the body; if sufficient is not available, the reserves held in the collagen have to go, heralding softer muscles, looser hips and, surprisingly enough, HD. This could account for many hip problems caused by loose femoral heads in the acetabuli.

Why, you may ask, do some breeds and lines have more trouble than others? A Swedish vet, Dr Stenn-Erik Olssen, observed that it was almost impossible to damage a Greyhound's hips. The Greyhound can be run or raced and, in the tradition of wheel-backed type dogs, finish smiling. Many regard this breed as having the best hips in the world. Dr Olssen bred one of these dogs to a line of German Shepherds with a bad record of HD. By careful selective breeding, he produced a dog with the physical appearance (phenotype) of a German Shepherd and the genotypical hips of a Greyhound. This dog was identifiable to the eye as a German Shepherd; however, under the disguise were the hips of a typical Greyhound.

The moral here is that a German Shepherd with hips very susceptible to HD because of its breed now had hips free of problems because of a Greyhound that was not susceptible. In other words, if hips not susceptible to HD are transposed to a breed that is susceptible, the best of both worlds is achieved.

Expounding this a little further, the German Shepherd by the very presence of his DNA molecules would always produce hips of a German Shepherd. Like the heavier dogs mentioned earlier this dog had not become extinct. The genes that had been responsible for these hips for thousands of years were obviously producing hips suitable for this breed's size, weight and use. Why would the hips break down and cease to fulfil their intended function? Could it be that the hips were exposed to a set of conditions not foreseen by nature in the gradual evolvement and natural selection of the breed? Referring to the heavier Mastiff breeds, these have evolved over the centuries more or less as they were in the days when Julius Caesar invaded Britain. Why do we see so many problems in the last few decades? Could it be that the environmental stress on the genotypical hips of the breed is too severe for its original use in today's society? The dog's hips are fine, the dog is fine, but the daily stress of noise and fast society remove too much sodium ascorbate from the collagen, putting too much demand on the hips found in a majority of that breed.

Critics will say that some lines seem to be completely free of HD. This statement can be viewed with some scepticism. To those who seem to escape most of the time, consider the dark past of your line at the turn of the century. Is it possible that you were fortunate enough to inherit a line whose hips were selected to cope in a society 50 years down the road or did some shrewd breeder of old sneak in a Greyhound type or two?

It seems safe to say that, after the exhaustive activity of the Swedish army to remove HD from their dogs by severe and persistent culling, HD still appeared. The opinion at that time was that the HD was being controlled by a wild gene and could not be identified or subdued by man. Maybe the solution to finding this wild gene was always present depending on where the observer was looking and under whose guidance. Maybe the seekers were looking in the wrong place. Everyone was looking for a gene because they had been told to look for a gene. Maybe, just maybe, it was not the fault of the gene but of the environment. Such a hypothesis is hard to prove or disprove because of the money, facilities and size of cross-section needed for such testing. Maybe it's time to look at this problem from a different direction and examine new ideas about this subject which has eluded man up until now. It is always easier to cling to the side you know than strike out into deep water and the unknown but how else will the swimmer and this noble breed of Bullmastiffs survive? One Titanic is enough!

Eventide

A medieval Saxon Baron was once sitting in his large hall having a feast with his friends, as Saxon Barons were wont to do, when a bird flew in from the dark, flitted briefly around the hall and disappeared again out into the inky night. Upon seeing this the Baron, who was usually considered a hard, insensitive person, reflected that the bird's action was a picture of life. We come from who knows where? We appear briefly on the scene of life, and then disappear just who knows where? In the millenniums of life our brief appearance is no longer than the bird's in the hall light.

The life span of a Bullmastiff is but a short 10 years or less, a possible 15% of the average human being's. When the time comes to fly back out into the night the way is not always clear; sometimes the exit is blocked by ignorance, insensitivity or, still worse, negligence.

Bullmastiffs are dogs with pride, loyalty, bravery and fidelity. Sometimes they do not know they are hurting or that they did not always walk the way they do today because of physical disabilities. Sometimes they just do not want to find the way out of the light even when they know it is high time. This is when you as a considerate owner must make the decision that will be hard to live with for many years after, but which must be faced. One thing you must remember is to let your Bullmastiff retain his pride and dignity to the very last. Be gentle and kind, but show him the way out of the hall into the darkness beyond in a way that he will thank you for, so that you can be content in your mind that it was the right time.

Let the dog's quality of life always be your guide.

Above left:Bullmastiffs enjoying another form of exercise - swimming.
Above right: Nothing wrong with me!

Above left & right: even having a leg amputated to try to halt the spread of cancer did not prevent this bitch from leading a full life. Unfortunately, the cancer spread and owners Brenda and Ian Ball made the decision to have her put to sleep.

CHAPTER TEN

Famous Bullmastiffs In Britain

Ch Bunsoro Dianna.

Bulldog: Ch Pugilist, one of the top CC winners between the Wars.

This section was compiled by Dr Desirée Scott, breed historian.

Introduction

Dogs of Bullmastiff type had existed for many years before the start of dog shows. The Kennel Club was founded in 1873 to bring some rules to bear in the rather shady occupation of dog shows, and brought out their Stud Book the next year. This book was a record of the prize-winning dogs at the biggest of shows from 1859 to 1873, and has been followed with a volume every year since.

The show prize lists for the 19th century occasionally included the winners of a class for 'Gamekeepers' Night Dogs', a common name for the Bullmastiff in pre-recognition years.

Kennel Club
Recognition and the First Challenge Certificates

In 1924 the breed was recognised by The Kennel Club, with the spelling Bull-Mastiff (Pure bred), and with particular attention to be paid to 'the distinction between a Bull-Mastiff pure bred, and a Bull-Mastiff cross bred, the former being a dog bred with both parents and the preceding three generations all Bull-Mastiffs without the introduction of a Mastiff or a Bulldog. The term Bull Mastiff cross bred implies the existence of a definite cross which has not yet been bred out.'

Farcroft Fidelity.

Ch Roger of the Fenns.

The first Crufts classes were in 1926 when Mr Moseley's Farcroft Fidelity was the winner of Best of Breed. As outlined in Chapter 2, Mr Moseley believed in Mastiff/Bulldog crosses and rigorously avoided using anything else. The head of the Bulldog at the beginning of the 20th century was (and still is) very different from that of the Mastiff. The Bulldog's muzzle is much shorter, with a much more defined stop, and the mandible (the bone that forms the underjaw) is longer than the bones that form the upper portion of the jaw. Due to the differences in the length of the two parts of the jaw, the lower jaw sweeps upwards for the teeth to meet.

The Mastiff has a very large head, with equal length of the bones that form the muzzle, a head type that is much more 'normal'. The head that was aimed at for

Mastiff: Ch Crown Prince.

the Bullmastiff was one between these two, but many Bullmastiffs had heads that erred to either Bulldog or Mastiff type. This legacy still exists in the show ring today, with heads of a multitude of types still appearing.

Existing photographs of Mr Moseley's dogs, including Fidelity, show dogs with a head structure more in the Mastiff mould than we would like today, and Fidelity was criticised by contemporary breeders for his weak muzzle and poor ear carriage. A wise man once said to me that the ancestors of a breed can be seen in the faults that the breeder tries to eradicate. Finality had the rose ear carriage of his Bulldog forebears and the muzzle of the Mastiff ones, exactly the opposite of what was intended, but he looks a dog of sound construction with hindquarters that his breeder considered 'would not disgrace an Alsatian' (German Shepherd). Soundness has always been a problem in breeds of Mastiff descent, so his array of show wins (he retired unbeaten) seems most likely to be due to the fact that his plain head was well compensated for by construction far superior to that of any of his contemporaries.

The first set of Challenge Certificates for the breed were on offer at Crufts in February 1928. The dog CC was won by Mr Victor J Smith's homebred Tiger Prince, whose sire Tiger Torus was a son of Fidelity, but whose dam had no Farcroft breeding in her rather short pedigree. All of her grandparents were unregistered with The Kennel Club. The bitch CC was won by Mr Moseley's brindle bitch Farcroft Silvo, who had been Best of Breed the year before without Certificates. She was a brindle whose head seems to have been stronger than that of her kennel mate, Fidelity.

The next pair of CCs on offer were at the Manchester Show at the end of March and, whilst Tiger Prince had to stand third in the Open Dog class, Silvo took her second CC. The dog CC winner was Mrs J Murray Smith's Athos, a son of Fidelity who had been second to Tiger Prince at Crufts.

The third set of Bull Mastiff (Pure bred) CCs was awarded at the 1928 Kennel Club show, held at its regular time in October. The dog placings were a repeat of Manchester, with Tiger Prince taking his second CC, and Farcroft Silvo winning the third bitch CC to become the very first Bullmastiff champion. Her position of dominance was confirmed when she won the last CC of the year at Birmingham National show just before Christmas. The judge was Count V C Hollander, whose own breed was the Bull Terrier but who had been a long-time admirer of the Bullmastiff, having written a magazine article in 1911 on this 'unrecognised breed of British dogs'.

The dog CC winner under the Count was Fidelity himself, with Tiger Prince in third place in the Open Dog class to one of his sons. Silvo ended the year as the only champion made up, and the top winning dog was Tiger Prince who had two CCs.

An outstanding Bullmastiff head. Note: muzzle longer than in Bulldog but shorter than in Mastiff.

Top: Ch Frederick of Kelwall, memorable for the fine movement he passed on to his offspring.
Bottom: Ch Bonnie of Kelwall, the first Brindle champion in the breed.

At Crufts 1929 Mr Moseley's dogs won the two premier awards, Farcroft Finality (grandson of Fidelity) won his first CC and Silvo continued her unbroken run of awards. The next Bull Mastiff (Pure bred) CCs were on offer at Manchester, and Ch Farcroft Silvo did not win the bitch CC! The winner was Mr J and Mr T W Barnard's Princess Betty, a daughter of Finality out of a bitch who was the granddaughter of a champion Mastiff (Ch King Baldur).

The first male champion and, indeed, the first fawn champion was made up on 20 March 1929 at Manchester, and this was Ch Tiger Prince. He won his fourth CC at Worcester and District Canine Society in August (this show is no longer a championship one). He was bred and owned by Mr Victor Smith, who had been attracted to the breed when a lady and her Bullmastiff moved in over the road from him. After an incident when an unwelcome caller was escorted from those premises by the Bullmastiff, both Mr Smith and his wife decided this was the breed for them. At this time, many dogs were carried unaccompanied on trains, so their bitch puppy, Princess Poppy, arrived at the station in a tea chest, greeting them with a display of her dentition when the lid was removed! They decided to have a litter from her and looked for a suitable dog. Finding an advertisement in a newspaper they travelled on motorbike and side car to the address given, a fish and chip shop up a Birmingham back street. They were happy with the dog, Tiger Torus, and having settled the price Mrs Smith negotiated him into the side car and then travelled home as a pillion passenger. The subsequent mating produced Tiger Prince.

The last two shows of the year (and the most prestigious) were The Kennel Club Show - where the secretary of The Kennel Club, Mr Croxton Smith, was judging - and Birmingham National Show, which had been around 13 years before The Kennel Club was formed. The Farcrofts were successful at both of these, Silvo won both Bitch CCs and Finality won the two Dog ones to gain his title. Silvo finished with 14 CCs, the breed record until well into the 1950s. Four of her CCs were won at Crufts.

Lack of space prevents me from covering the entire history of the breed in detail, so I have chosen to focus on the top stud dogs.

Top Bullmastiff Stud Dogs

Ch Roger of the Fenns: 10 champions
Ch Billy of Stanfell: 10 champions
Ch Branch of Bulmas: 9 champions
Ch Oldwell Toby of Studbergh: 9 champions
Azer of Oldwell: 9 champions
Ch Loki of Mulorna: 8 champions
Ch Sharwells Mean Mr Mustard of Pitmans: 8 champions
Ch Nicholas of Oldwell: 7 champions
Ch Ambassador of Buttonoak: 6 champions
Ch Bulstaff Achilles: 5 champions

Ch Roger of the Fenns: top pre-war stud dog

The top stud dog pre-war was Ch Roger of the Fenns, who was bred by Mr G F Wedgewood in 1929, and owned by Mr J Toney. His sire, Don Juan, was a grandson of Farcroft Fidelity and had a line to the Mastiff Ch King Baldur as well, and his dam was a daughter of Ch Tiger Prince. Roger won two Crufts CCs, as did one of his predecessors (Ch King Baldur's dam, Ch Young Mary Bull, won the bitch CCs in 1916 and 1922).

His record of 10 champion offspring means that he is joint top sire, together with the leading post-war sire, Ch Billy of Stanfell, in the breed's history. Not only did Roger sire so many champions, but they included dogs of truly outstanding head construction that helped to stabilise breed type. His own muzzle was a little longer than is now considered typical but his sons, Ch Billy of Bulmas and Ch Beppo of Bulmas, were very typey indeed.

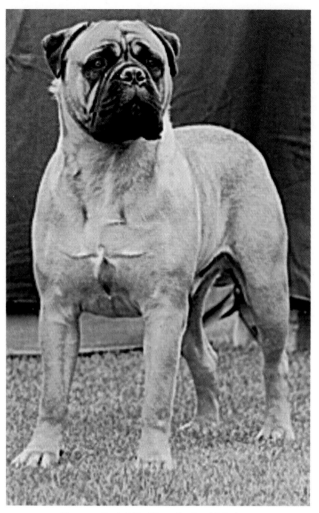

Bunsoro Red Sails. Photo by David Dalton.

Ch Billy of Stanfell: top post-war stud dog

Mr and Mrs Higginson's Stanfells started in 1928. The first champion they bred was Ch Beppica of Bulmas, a daughter of Ch Beppo. At this time the rules for registration and names were much less strict than now; a complete change of name was permissible so that is why Beppica did not have the affix Stanfell in her name.

As well as breeding and owning the first post-war bitch champion, the Higginson's also bred and owned the first post-war dog champion, Ch Boy of Stanfell. Indeed, the first nine post-war champions had a Stanfell parent. The most influential of the Stanfells was Ch Billy of Stanfell, who was born in 1943 and was a grandson of Ch Roger of the Fenns through his sire Ch Springwell Simba. Simba was one of the last Bullmastiff champions made up pre-war as he gained his title in 1939.

Ch Billy of Stanfell equalled the 10 champions sired by his grandfather to become the leading post-war sire. His first champion offspring won her title a year before her sire in 1947, and the last of his children to win their title was Ch Radcot Classic who gained his third CC in 1953.

Ch Branch of Bulmas: sire of nine champions

Another top sire was Ch Branch of Bulmas with his nine champion offspring winning their titles between 1948 and 1952. Ch Branch was a son of Bonnie of Stanfell, a sister of Ch Beauty of Stanfell which demonstrates how closely Bulmas and Stanfell were working together. They were both aiming for a dog with elegance, substance and a good strong head. Mr Higginson was determined through his breeding and judging to remove the weak 'Dane-like' head from the breed.

The Bulmas affix is one of the greatest in the breed and spanned the Second World War. Mr Cyril Leeke returned from distinguished service during the First World War to an economic situation much different from a country 'fit for heroes' that had been promised. In the early 1920s he was dejectedly having lunch at a public house when he heard a deep resounding 'woof' from the back. He felt that this sound touched him inside and, on enquiring from the landlord what the dog's breed was, he found it to be a Bullmastiff. There and then he decided he must have a dog like it and bought a bitch who was to be the foundation of his line in partnership with Mrs Hill. After much thought about an affix he suddenly realised that simply shortening the breed's name gave a distinctive word. So Sheila of Bulmas was registered and, when she was mated to the Farcroft-bred Ch Peter of the Fenns, she produced the first Bulmas champion in 1921. This was Ch Wendy of

Bulmas. When the latter was mated to Ch Roger of the Fenns, she produced Ch Billy of Bulmas and Ch Beppo of Bulmas in the same litter. The Second World War prevented either of these brothers having a proper stud career. Ch Billy had a champion son, whilst Ch Beppo produced two champion daughters before the war, plus the first post-war champion, Ch Beauty of Stanfell.

Though the Bulmas dogs were important for the breed, they were not perfect. In his excellent book on Mastiffs and Bullmastiffs, Mr Douglas Oliff says

> *...the strain was not faultless, light eyes bedevilled it, and mouths were not always good as irregular placement of the front teeth of the lower jaw occurred from time to time. Hind angulation could have been better in some of the big winners, but taken as a whole Bulmas combined true type with size and overall quality.*

The Bulmas dogs were similar in appearance to each other during times where there were many types around, and this appearance was of a very good Bullmastiff indeed. The stud dogs from the kennel did much for the breed by producing high quality stock of the type other breeders were struggling to produce.

The last Bulmas champion was Ch Beauty of Bulmas, the Crufts CC winner of 1957. Later that year, Mr Leeke and his kennel left for the United States. The venture was not a successful one, but Mr Leeke and his second wife Mary stayed out there during the lifetime of Ch Beauty as they did not want her to pass into other hands.

Part of the kennel's success in the ring was Mr Leeke's wonderful rapport with each dog so that it showed its best for him. He could show both greedy dogs and poor feeders; in the ring the greedy dog would wait most attentively for the sound of a scrunched-up paper, believing a piece of liver was just about to appear.

Ch Bombadillo of Bunsoro.

Ch Coldstream of Bunsoro (sire: Ch Bombadillo of Bunsoro).

Top: Ch Doomwatch Gipsy of Oldwell.
Bottom: Ch Little Miss of Oldwell, Crufts Best Of Breed 1968.

Ch Oldwell Toby of Studbergh and Azer of Oldwell: sires of nine champions

Two other dogs hold the record of siring nine champions, and they came from the same kennel; the phenomenally successful Oldwell kennel of Harry and Beryl Collias. In 1937 they saw an advertisement in a newspaper for a Bullmastiff, and this started a lifelong 'affair' with the breed. After the war they decided to breed top quality Bullmastiffs, and started with a dog and a bitch from two of the most famous bloodlines. The dog was Ace of Buttonoak, and the wisdom of this purchase became evident when he sired the first Oldwell champion, Ch Bambino.

The dam of Ch Bambino was Mayqueen of Marbetta, from the kennel of Mrs E B Millard and Mrs M Eaton. Their first champion was Ch Master of Marbette, the result of a Stanfell/Bulmas breeding. At first Mrs Millard felt that it would be a mistake to mate her to a Buttonoak dog because the lines were so different, but when she saw she was mistaken she mated Mayqueen's litter sister to Ace's litter brother and produced two dog champions.

By 1991 the Oldwell kennel had produced 51 champions and had extensive influence through its stud dogs, Ch Oldwell Toby of Studbergh sired nine champions who gained their titles from 1967 to 1970; in 1968 he was the sire of all five of the Bullmastiff champions to be made up that year. Both his parents were Marbettes (Ch Master Brandy of Marbette x Miss Polly of Marbette) and his grandsire was Ch Mi Brandy of Marbette, one Mrs Millard's 'experimental' champion dogs.

Azer of Oldwell never gained his title but he also sired nine champions. The first was Ch Doomwatch Gypsy of Oldwell, who gained her title in 1974 and the last was Ch Naukeen Leila, in 1978. Azer was placed in a few Open Dog classes at championship shows, so he did gain his stud book number. His sire, Ch Regent of Oldwell, was a son of Ch Oldwell Toby of Studbergh.

Ch Loki of Mulorna: sire of eight champions

Two of the top stud dogs we have discussed so far were around at the same time; both Ch Branch of Bulmas and Ch Billy of Stanfell were siring the champions of the late 1940s and early 1950s. There was also another excellent stud dog around at this time: Mrs Doris Mullin's Ch Loki of Mulorna. The Bullmastiff was not as badly affected after the war as its cousin, the Mastiff (when their numbers were counted at the end of hostilities, there were only seven left, and most of those were too old to breed from). The Bullmastiffs also had the advantage that, during this time of reconstruction, three of the all-time greats were available at stud. There are many people in the breed today who would give almost anything to have the choice of three outstanding stud dogs for their bitches.

Ch Loki was a rich mahogany red in colour, as was his sire Rhodian, who was robbed of his show career by the war. He won one CC in 1939, aptly enough at The Big Breeds Show. His grandsire was Mrs Mullin's first champion, Ch Tenz, who gained his title in 1934, and whom Mr Douglas Oliff considered as the progenitor of the Mulorna head and expression, an expression that looked at you and through you. His pedigree contained Tiger Torus and a number of Farcrofts.

The first of Loki's champion offspring was Ch Duchess of Stanfell, whose title in 1948 came a year before that of her sire. The last of his champion offspring was Ch St David of Gwydyr, bred at Mulorna but owned by Mr and Mrs Morris. He gained his title in 1957.

Ch Sharwell Mean Mr Mustard of Pitmans: sire of eight champions

This dog was born in 1983, gaining his title in 1985 and taking a total of 12 CCs. He was bred by Mr and Mrs Bakewell, but was owned by Mr and Mrs Leeson whose Pitman's kennel had bred his sire, Ch Pitman's Deputy. Deputy was a son of Ch Pitman's Buccaneer, whose sire was the Crufts group winning Ch Craigylea Sir Galahad. Bullmastiffs rarely win groups, especially at the top championship shows, for often these are judged by all-rounder judges who lay more emphasis on good construction and movement than specialist breed points. Bullmastiff movement is often not as good as that of other breeds in the group.

The 1977 Crufts group judge was Mr Percy Whittaker, who wrote:

The supreme placing went to the Bullmastiff. I cannot remember for some time seeing such a happy and alert specimen. I shall long remember his great stance, faultless front, his lovely ears, his great strength without coarseness, and who has ever seen such a beautiful neck? An outstanding group, headed by an equally outstanding dog.

Sir Galahad was a son of Ch Pitman's Gentleman Jim, who had himself been a Crufts Best of Breed winner (1972) but tragically died as a very young dog from heatstroke. His sire, Bulstaff Turvey, was an untitled dog who was, nevertheless, a phenomenal sire. In 1971 five Bullmastiff champions were made up and Turvey sired four of these. They were not 'ordinary' champions either; as well as Gentleman Jim, he sired Ch Pekingtown Abece who won three Crufts CCs amongst her total of 19, and is considered by Mrs Lynn Pratt, one of the most distinguished of breeders, as the best ever bitch in the breed:

She was a beautiful pale fawn, ideal size, excellent bone, front and shoulders with strong muscular quarters.

Turvey's sire was Ch Bulstaff Achilles, of whom more later.

Ch Nicholas of Oldwell: sire of seven champions

The dog that is eighth in the list of all-time great stud dogs in the Bullmastiff is another from the Oldwell kennel, Ch Nicholas of Oldwell. He was born in 1971, by Ch Thorfin of Oldwell x Bridget of Oldwell. Mr Colliass considered that Thorfin was possibly one of the best of the Oldwells, but he died very young, before he was fully mature, having gained his title aged two. Thorfin was a son of Ch Regent of Oldwell who was sired by the previously discussed Ch Oldwell Toby of Studbergh.

The first champion that Nicholas sired was a bitch who not only won 13 CCs but was considered one of the very best of her breed. Mr William Newton of the Galastock Bullmastiffs has done much to publish historic photographs from Mr Colliass' collection. He had a particularly soft spot for this bitch, Ch Honeybee of Oldwell, writing:

Not only was she a paragon in the aesthetic sense, but her attributes, in my opinion, encompassed the complete essence of the breed requirements. Many Bullmastiffs have almost matched the mathematical blueprint, the Standard, but few have combined all the required elements of matching a correct physical appearance with an equally impressive, extrovert, yet loving and tolerant personality She did!

Her dam was St Mungo Minerva, a daughter of Ch Pitmans Gentleman Jim, and the mating of Ch Nicholas to Minerva was carried out three times, producing six champions:

Ch Honeybee of Oldwell (13CCs including two at Crufts)
Ch Verona of Oldwell (11 CCs)
Ch Frazer of Oldwell (8CCs)
Ch Kracka of Oldwell (8 CCs)
Ch Crystal of Oldwell (13 CCs)

Though all these puppies were registered as Oldwells, they were bred by Dr and Mrs Fraser.

Ch Ambassador of Buttonoak: sire of six champions

Mr and Mrs Terry had founded their Buttonoak kennel on Bulmas lines, their foundation bitch being Ch Bimbi of Bulmas 'a lovely clear fawn with perfect pigmentation of good size with perfect balance who always moved well'. She was the winner of 11 CCs, including Crufts in 1951 and 1952.

The first Buttonoak champion was her son, Ch Anthony of Buttonoak, followed by his litter brother, Ch Caesar of Buttonoak. Anthony was often considered by some breed specialists as the

Susan Cox and Colom Okeechobee
Photo: Bull

greatest from this kennel. However he was overshadowed by his kennelmate, Ch Ambassador of Buttonoak, the favourite of all-round judges because of the verve and style he had, in addition to his good breed points. Ambassador was also the litter brother of Ace of Buttonoak, the Oldwell foundation stud; Ambassador was the stud dog used by Mrs Millard to produce two Marbetta champions from the litter sister of Mayqueen of Marbetta, the Oldwell foundation bitch.

Ambassador was reserve Best in Show on the second day of Crufts in 1956. At this time there was no group judging at Crufts; all the Best of Breed winners on the first day competed for Best of Show that day, and the process was repeated the second day leaving two dogs to compete for the title of Best in Show (Crufts was a two day show at that time).

When I was at school I was given an old copy of the 1957 Crufts catalogue and I was fascinated by the way breeds had altered from that date. In many breeds the dogs of 1957 had much less coat, or different styles of presentation, but there was also the much more serious fault of less sound construction than was generally the case in the 1970s. There was one exception to this, the Bullmastiff whose photograph opened the section on the breed. This was the first time I saw a photograph of Ch Ambassador of Buttonoak and my breath was quite taken away by the dog's soundness, his wonderful topline and good head. It seemed that he would not have looked out of place in the rings of the 1970s. This picture is indelibly imprinted on my mind.

Ambassador was by Ch Rodenhurst Masterpiece x Ch Swatchway Amethyst of Buttonoak, a daughter of the first post-war dog champion, Ch Boy of Stanfell. His most illustrious son was Ch Ambassadorson of Buttonoak, who was reserve Best in Show at Crufts in 1958 and whose own son, Ch Alaric of Buttonoak, was Best in Show at Birmingham City Champion Show in 1958. Ambassadorson was out of the bitch Angela of Buttonoak, a daughter of the Buttonoak foundation Ch Bimbi of Bulmas.

Ch Bulstaff Achilles: sire of five champions

Another fine son of Ch Ambassador of Buttonoak was Ch Bulstaff Brobdingnag. He is remembered not so much for winning four CCs, but as the sire of the breed record holder Ch Bulstaff Achilles. Achilles' record of 24 CCs was gained in the 1960s when there were far fewer CCs available than is the case now. Amongst these were three won at Crufts.

He was bred by Ralph and Ruth Short, who kept their Bulstaff dogs as house pets rather than as kennel dogs. When Achilles was eight weeks old they had a fire which caused quite a bit of damage. Achilles was going to be the puppy kept and run on from the two litters that had just been born, but the fire meant that no puppies could stay, and he went to his new home. Mr and Mrs Short had considered the Achilles litter to be especially nice so, when his new owner phoned six months later to say she had just had a major operation and could not cope with an exuberant male Bullmastiff, he came home.

His excellent breed points were augmented by a lovely personality and great showmanship. His movement was outstanding, and many have written about his outstanding head: 'a *classic head with really dark ears*', '*great strength of muzzle with a level bite*', '*just the right length of muzzle*', '*it would be difficult to fault this dog*'.

He was retired at the age of five as the Shorts were rapidly losing their friends! All his CCs were won under different judges, except on one occasion when there was a last-minute substitution. He came out two years later for a couple of new judges. Although he sired five champions, this number would surely have been greater if he had not become sterile at the height of his stud career. This was thought to be caused by an infection picked up from a visiting bitch.

Ch Ambassador of Buttonoak.

Ch Todomas Tanya of Bunsoro.

Name	Sex	DOB	Sire	Dam	Breeder	Owner	CCs
1928							
Ch Farcroft Silvo	b	18.03.25	Hamil Grip	Farcroft Belltong	S E Moseley	Breeder	14
1929							
Ch Tiger Prince	d	21.06.25	Tiger Torus	Princess Poppy	V J Smith	Breeder	4
Ch Farcroft Finality	d	09.06.27	Farcroft Fidelity's Filius	Farcroft Fealty	S E Moseley	Breeder	6
1931							
Ch Farcroft Felon's Frayeur	d	01.09.27	Farcroft Faction	Farcroft Fend	S E Moseley	Breeder	3
1932							
Ch Athos	d	22.09.26	Farcroft Fidelity	Noble	The Hon Mrs J Murray-Smith	Breeder	3
Ch Farcroft Fabric	b	26.06.31	Ch Farcroft Finality	Ch Farcroft Silvo	S E Moseley	Breeder	4
Ch Peter of the Fenns	d	14.04.28	Farcroft Formative	Farcroft Staunch	S E Moseley	J E V Toney	3
Ch Simba	d	28.06.29	Ch Athos	Lady Athena	G Pollard	The Marquis of Londonderry	6
1933							
Ch Roger of the Fenns	d	07.11.29	Don Juan	Luzlow Princess	G F Wedgewood	J E V Toney	6
Ch Bubbles	b	14.07.30	Ch Farcroft Felon's Frayeur	Lady Betty of Bowdencourt	D Hardman Darbyshire	T Pennington	4
Ch Sans Faut	d	24.06.29	Bullers Fidelity	Wingates Pride	G Bullough	W Crumble Hulme	4
Ch Castlecroft Peggy Ann	b	03.04.30	Ch Farcroft Finality	Rosland Felice	Mrs Rose	Miss J Lane	3
1934							
Ch Tenz	d	12.08.31	Vindictive Prince	Princess Ursula	J & T W Bernard & Mrs D Mullin	Mrs D Mullin	3
Ch Jeanie of Wynyard	b	12.04.31	Ch Simba	Fruach of Ranald	The Marquis of Londonderry	The Hon Mrs J Murray-Smith	9
Ch Wendy of Bulmas	b	18.07.31	Ch Peter of the Fenns	Sheila of Bulmas	Mrs G E Hill & C R Leeke	Breeders	5
Ch Wisdom of Wynyard	d	24.03.32	Ch Simba	Fruach of Ranald	The Marquis of Londonderry	L Edwards	7
1935							
Ch Torfrida of the Fenns	b	25.10.32	Ch Roger of the Fenns	Poppy of the Fenns	J E V Toney	Breeder	3

Name	Sex	DOB	Sire	Dam	Breeder	Owner	CCs
Ch Billy of Bulmas	d	21.08.33	Ch Roger of the Fenns	Ch Wendy of Bulmas	Mrs G E Hill & C R Leeke	Breeders	5
1936							
Ch Bartonville Red Sultan	d	21.04.32	Pridzor King	Ch Bubbles	T Pennington	E Massie	3
Ch Mackwyn Excelsior	d	27.12.32	Major of Kalka	Lady of Kalka	A Rix	Miss E P Marsh	3
Ch Silbrin	b	22.02.32	Pridzor King	Duchess May	Mr & Mrs S Rogers	Mrs E Smith	3
Ch Beppo of Bulmas	d	21.08.33	Ch Roger of the Fenns	Ch Wendy of Bulmas	Mrs G E Hill & C R Leeke	J Higginson	12
Ch Roger of Brooklands	d	01.04.34	Ch Roger of the Fenns	Ch Bubbles	T Pennington	E L Spruce	7
Ch Potters Pride	b	24.05.33	Vindictive Prince	More Tuns Princess	J Moreton	D Guthrie	5
1937							
Ch Rosland Felice	b	14.04.28	Farcroft Formative	Farcroft Staunch	S E Moseley	Miss M Rose	3
Ch Arpens Peterpenn	b	05.04.36	Arpens Golden Lion	Bringold Queen of Arpens	A Pennington	Breeder	3
Ch Sealton Janet	b	26.07.36	Ch Beppo of Bulmas	Freda of Stanfell	E Burton	Miss B A Cain	5
1938							
Ch Beppica of Bulmas	b	25.08.35	Ch Beppo of Bulmas	Jessica of the Fenns	J Higginson	Mrs G E Hill & C R Leeke	4
Ch Springwell Major	d	20.10.35	Ch Roger of the Fenns	Lady Dinah of Springwell	W & G K Richardson	Breeders	5
Ch Spotless Lady	b	12.10.34	Ch Roger of the Fenns	Nita	Capt C Towler	Miss D McLean	3
Ch Modjosa (Late Chestonian Staunch)	b	01.01.36	Palmerston King	Jose's Pride	Mrs A Tunnicliffe	A Moody	3
Ch Bartonville Grand Parade	d	01.04.34	Ch Roger of the Fenns	Ch Bubbles	T Pennington	F Cooke	3
Ch Navigation Terror	d	31.10.35	Ch Billy of Bulmas	Navigation Lady Maysi	E Burton	Breeder	4
Ch Millbrook Peter	d	20.10.35	Ch Roger of the Fenns	Lady Dinah of Springwell	W & G K Richardson	B Kennedy	4
Ch Red Nell of Conheath	b	16.07.35	Red Rufus	Nell	J C Macintyre	E Clark	6
1939							
Ch Tenas	b	21.03.35	Ch Tenz	Lady Tess	A Moody	Breeder	4
Ch Jeanette of Brooklands	b	01.01.34	Ch Roger of the Fenns	Ch Bubbles	T Pennington	E L Spruce	3
Ch Springwell Simba	d	05.03.37	Ch Roger of the Fenns	Springwell Lady Tessa	W & G K Richardson	R S Critchley	4
Ch Bobby of Tunshill	d	19.08.37	Ch Arpens Peterpenn	Lady Betty of Bilson	Mrs E Tonge	Breeder	3

Name	Sex	DOB	Sire	Dam	Breeder	Owner	CCs
Ch Yvette of Brooklands	b	17.03.37	Ch Roger of Brooklands	Paulette of Brooklands	E L Spruce	Breeder	3
1947							
Ch Beauty of Stanfell	b	17.07.41	Ch Beppo of Bulmas	Bits of Stanfell	J Higginson	Breeder	3
Ch Boy of Stanfell	d	16.08.45	Hickathrift RA of Tasyll	Blossom of Stanfell	J Higginson	Breeder	6
Ch Carrokid Dawn	b	07.05.45	Ch Billy of Stanfell	Dellabess	R Carter	Mr & Mrs R Carter	6
1948							
Ch Billy of Stanfell	d	14.07.43	Ch Springwell Simba	Bessie of Stanfell	J Higginson	T Avery	3
Ch Betty of Goodyear	b	29.11.44	Hickathrift RA of Tasyll	Babs of Stanfell	T F Akerman	V Smith	3
Ch Magician of Bablock	d	04.05.46	Ch Billy of Stanfell	Sally of Bablock	T Avery	C Clark	5
Ch Branch of Bulmas	d	08.12.44	Beefy of Bulmas	Bonnie of Stanfell	C R Leeke	Breeder	3
Ch Jill of Lisvane	b	31.10.46	Ch Billy of Stanfell	Judy of Lisvane	Mrs M Sparkes	Breeder	3
Ch Duchess of Stanfell	b	22.09.46	Ch Loki of Mulorna	Blossom of Stanfell	J Higginson	W Burgess	3
Ch Bulldozer of Bulmas	d	22.06.46	Ch Branch of Bulmas	Bronwen of Bulwyn	Mrs E D Atkinson & C R Leeke	N Moor	3
1949							
Ch Bimbi of Bulmas	b	26.02.48	Ch Branch of Bulmas	Bronzy of Bulmas	C R Leeke	Mr & Mrs E L Terry	11
Ch Loki of Mulorna	d	17.06.41	Rhodian	Meg of Mulorna	Mrs D Mullin	Breeder	3
Ch Barney of Valdor	d	15.10.47	Ch Billy of Stanfell	Jose of Valdor	V Tasker	Mrs D Tasker	3
Ch Billagain of Bulmas	d	16.07.47	Ch Boy of Stanfell	Baggage of Bulmas	C R Leeke	Breeder	4
Ch Maritime Juliet	b	23.05.48	Maritime Fearless	Tula of Denham	W H Medhurst	Mrs M E Lewis	7
Ch Buddy of Hickathrift	d	21.06.47	Ch Loki of Malorna	Hickathrift Paddy of Le Tasyll	A E Taylor	A E Taylor & Mrs D Mullin	3
1950							
Ch Master of Marbette	d	16.04.48	Ch Boy of Stanfell	Berwyn of Bulmas	Mmes E B Millard & K C Eaton	Breeders	3
Ch Grantirk Griffin	d	15.08.48	Ch Loki of Mulorna	Grantirk Pandora	W T East	Breeder	3
Ch Battleroyal of Bulmas	b	30.04.48	Ch Branch of Bulmas	By Chance of Bulmas	C R Leeke	Breeder	4
Ch Robin Hood of Le Tasyll	d	16.01.45	Hickathrift RA of Tasyll	Rosland Diana of Le Tasyll	Mrs D J Nash	Breeder	3
Ch Beppicagain of Bulmas	b	16.07.47	Ch Boy of Stanfell	Baggage of Bulmas	C R Leeke	Breeder	3
Ch Madame Rouge	b	12.03.48	Barrakhuta Warrior	Clarissa of Le Tasyll	K Jackson	Mrs V M Massie	5
Ch Rodenhurst Masterpiece	d	30.07.49	Rodenhurst Duke	Tasmar Daffodil	E L Spruce	Breeder	4

Name	Sex	DOB	Sire	Dam	Breeder	Owner	CCs
Ch Major of Stanfell	d	02.06.48	Ch Branch of Bulmas	Blossom of Stanfell	J Higginson	C Derwent	3
1951							
Ch Prizdor's Ideal	d	07.10.49	Ch Billy of Stanfell	Radcot Enterprise	Mr & Mrs C Clark	V Smith	6
Ch Grandtirk Grundy	d	25.03.49	Ch Branch of Bulmas	Grantirk Pandora	W T East	Breeder	7
Ch Bright Gem of Bulmas	b	07.09.49	Ch Branch of Bulmas	Ch Beppicagain of Bulmas	C R Leeke	Breeder	9
Ch Melody of Lisvane	b	28.11.48	Ch Bulldozer of Bulmas	Ch Jill of Lisvane	Mrs M Sparkes	Mrs T Storm	4
Ch Bruce of Radcot	d	07.10.49	Ch Billy of Stanfell	Radcot Enterprise	Mr & Mrs C Clark	Mrs L Matthews	4
Ch Brancella of Bulmas	b	16.11.48	Ch Branch of Bulmas	By Chance of Bulmas	C R Leeke	Mrs P D Garratt-Adams	3
Ch Chips of Harbex	d	02.09.49	Pearly King of Harbex	Ruella Frustration	Mr & Mrs G B Powell	Mrs F A Warren	4
Ch Graystan Replica	b	11.04.49	Ch Billy of Stanfell	Ch Duchess of Stanfell	W Burgess	Mrs A Bullough	3
Ch Prizdor's Reward	d	17.09.50	Ch Billy of Stanfell	Radcot Enterprise	Mr & Mrs C Clark	V Smith	13
1952							
Ch Tilly of Mara Lemac	b	18.11.46	Ch Loki of Mulorna	Tess of Werdna	A M Sommerville	Mrs A Mackie	3
Ch Wesgarth Black Magic	b	16.11.50	Ch Loki of Mulorna	Ch Madame Rouge	Mrs V M Massie	Breeder	8
Ch St Antony's Aristocrat	d	08.02.50	Rodenhurst Duke	Tasmar Daffodil	E L Spruce	I Forritt	4
Ch Rodenhurst Marksman	d	16.02.51	Ch Rodenhurst Masterpiece	Graystan Beauty	H E Marchington	E L Spruce	6
Ch Barnacle Bill of Bulmas	d	11.11.50	Ch Branch of Bulmas	Bonnie Judith of Bulmas	E White	C R Leeke	3
Ch Prizdor's Trust	b	17.09.50	Ch Billy of Stanfell	Radcot Enterprise	Mr & Mrs C Clark	V Smith	10
Ch Bulmas Maid Marion of Wyvern Hay	b	02.03.48	Ch Branch of Bulmas	Bairn of Bulmas	W H Killner	I Neers	3
1953							
Ch Bullseye of Bulmas	d	17.02.51	Ch Billagain of Bulmas	Beam of Bulmas	Mrs E Ball & W Martin	J Moss	4
Ch Sally Ann of Tip Dixon	b	04.11.49	Ch Loki of Mulorna	Cresta of Dixon	Miss F G Davis	Breeder	3
Ch Antony of Buttonoak	d	06.04.51	Bulmas Marco of Lisvane	Ch Bimbi of Bulmas	Mr & Mrs E L Terry	Breeders	4
Ch Swatchway Amethyst of Buttonoak	b	10.06.50	Ch Boy of Stanfell	Swatchway Model of Lisvane	Mrs S Arnold	Mr & Mrs E L Terry	4
Ch Radcot Classic	d	17.08.57	Ch Billy of Stanfell	Radcot Enterprise	Mr & Mrs C Clark	Breeders	8
1954							
Ch Caesar of Buttonoak	d	06.04.51	Bulmas Marco of Lisvane	Ch Bimbi of Bulmas	Mr & Mrs E L Terry	Mrs J D Wood	3

Name	Sex	DOB	Sire	Dam	Breeder	Owner	CCs
Ch Glamview Blazing Torch of Bulmas	b	16.11.52	Ch Caesar of Buttonoak	Baxy of Bulmas	C R Leeke	I Neers	3
Ch Buoyant of Bullturn	d	11.08.51	Prince of Purbeckdene	Beaufort of Bullturn	Mrs F Turnbull	Breeder	7
Ch Christina of Brixwood	b	10.12.51	Ch Loki of Mulorna	Cherie of Brixwood	Mr & Mrs T W Sutton	Breeders	6
Ch Duskie of Donegill	d	04.02.52	Ch Billagain of Bulmas	Bright Idea of Bulmas	D Robotham	Mr & Mrs D W Robotham	3
Ch Prizdor's Sweetheart	b	01.09.51	Ch Grantirk Grundy	Prizdor's Jewel	W Smith	T Waterfield	6
Ch Taffside Tarquin	d	21.06.52	Ch Prizdor's Reward	Ch Melody of Lisvane	Mrs T Storm	Breeder	3
Ch Bouncer of Bullturn	b	18.05.53	Ch Rodenhurst Marksman	Beaufort of Bullturn	Mrs F Turnbull	Breeder	14
1955							
Ch Ambassador of Buttonoak	d	03.05.53	Ch Rodenhurst Masterpiece	Ch Swatchway Amethyst of Buttonoak	Mr & Mrs E L Terry	Breeders	12
Ch Bluebell of Bullturn	b	14.02.53	Ch Buoyant of Bullturn	Bartica of Stanfell	J Higginson	Mrs F Turnbull	3
Ch Lanretta of Oakbank	b	10.06.53	Ch Rodenhurst Marksman	Rodenhurst Margo	L Charity	Breeder	6
Ch Goodstock Hunch of Gwydyr	d	07.04.54	Teddy of Lowston	Aster of Tafawen	C W Williams	Misses E P & L A Goodhall	6
1956							
Ch Bullbarrs Butch	d	26.04.54	Bullbarrs Brutus of Radcot	Bulways Bubbles	Mrs L Matthews	Breeder	4
Ch Mi Choice of Marbette	b	28.12.54	Midnight of Marbette	Miduchess of Marbette	S Smardon	Mmes E B Millard & M Eaton	3
1957							
Ch Beauty of Bulmas	b	07.08.54	Battlecry of Bulmas	Barney's Sister of Bulmas	C R Leeke	Breeder	3
Ch St David of Gwydyr	d	17.01.53	Ch Loki of Mulorna	Minx of Mulorna	Mrs D Mullin	Mr & Mrs W E Morris	3
Ch Bang On of Bulmas	d	05.08.52	Ch Barnacle Bill of Bulmas	Bulldena of Bulmas	C R Leeke	Mrs J J Elliot Smith	5
Ch Goodstock Trudy of Gwydyr	b	07.04.54	Teddy of Lowston	Aster of Tafawen	C W Williams	Misses E P & L A Goodhall	3
Ch Ambassadorson of Buttonoak	d	19.07.55	Ch Ambassador of Buttonoak	Angela of Buttonoak	Mr & Mrs E L Terry	Breeders	14
Ch Lincolnia of Leocon	b	18.11.55	Battlecry of Bulmas	Ballad of Bullturn	Mrs L Rhodes	Mr & Mrs L Rhodes	4
Ch Bambi of Stanfell	b	25.09.55	Ch Buoyant of Bullturn	Brumas of Stanfell	J Higginson	Breeder	7

149

Name	Sex	DOB	Sire	Dam	Breeder	Owner	CCs
Ch Cherie of Goodstock	b	07.04.54	Teddy of Lowston	Aster of Tafawen	C W Williams	Misses E P & L A Goodhall	4
1958							
Ch Tess of Ullapool	b	08.06.54	Goodstock Teddy of Lowston	Tawney Tanya	Mrs E Hankinson	Mrs J Pilling	3
Ch Mi Beauty of Marbette	b	04.09.56	Ch Master of Marbette	Mipal of Marbette	Mmes E B Millard & M Eaton	Breeders	3
Ch Alaric of Buttonoak	d	05.05.57	Ch Ambassadorson of Buttonoak	Bulstaff Heidi	Mr & Mrs J Bulman	Mrs F Willetts	3
Ch Mi Dinah of Marbette	b	04.09.56	Ch Master of Marbette	Mipal of Marbette	Mmes E B Millard & M Eaton	Mrs J Nago	3
1959							
Ch Goodstock Lord Joyful	d	02.06.53	Teddy of Lowston	Queen of Stockport	Misses E P & L A Goodhall	Breeders	4
Ch Marcus of Boaroy	d	26.10.55	Marcus of Mulorna	Lassie of Redhill	Mrs M E Keeling	Mrs R Boardman	6
Ch Bambino	b	21.02.57	Ace of Buttonoak	Mayqueen of Marbette	H Colliass	Breeder	6
Ch Alaro of Buttonoak	d	09.05.56	Ch Antony of Buttonoak	Avril of Buttonoak	Mr & Mrs E L Terry	Mrs J D Wood	7
Ch Bulstaff Prudence of Torhorwald	b	14.07.57	Bulstaff Jolly Roger	Bulstaff Puppa	Mrs S R Robinson	Mr & Mrs R E Short	5
1960							
Ch Ambrose of Edialhouse	d	27.11.56	Ch Ambassador of Buttonoak	Brigette of Bulmas	Mrs M Hammersley	M Byrnes	3
Ch Sweetie of Pillard	b	15.01.57	Ch Goodstock Lord Joyful	Ch Tess of Ullapool	Mrs W Pilling	Breeder	5
Ch Joyeuse of Goodstock	b	09.08.58	Ch Goodstock Lord Joyful	Goodstock Joyful Queen	Misses E P & L A Goodhall	Breeders	3
Ch Mi-Hope of Marbette	b	04.09.56	Ch Master of Marbette	Mipal of Marbette	Mmes E B Millard & M Eaton	Breeders	3
Ch Buttonoak Appeal of Gimingham	b	14.01.58	Ch Ambassadorson of Buttonoak	Betty's Beauty of Bulmas	Mrs M E Thomas	Mr & Mrs E L Terry	3
Ch Joyful Lass of Goodstock	b	30.06.59	Astleybridge Fast Lad	Lady Joyful of Goodstock	Misses E P & L A Goodhall	Mrs C Unsworth	6
Ch Oldwell Mi Trooper of Marbette	d	30.07.58	Ch Ambassador of Buttonoak	Ch Mi Choice of Marbette	Mmes E B Millard & M Eaton	H Colliass	5

Name	Sex	DOB	Sire	Dam	Breeder	Owner	CCs
1961							
Ch Romper Lad of Goodstock	d	30.06.59	Astleybridge Fast Lad	Lady Joyful of Goodstock	Misses E P & L A Goodhall	Mrs M Pope	5
Ch Romulus of Yotmas	d	18.03.57	Pridzor's Alibi	Gipsy of Marmast	J Martin	Mrs J J Elliot Smith	3
Ch Master Brandy of Marbette	d	07.01.60	Ch Mi Brandy of Marbette	Mi Penny of Marbette	Mmes E B Millard & M Eaton	Breeders	3
Ch Fromshane Strang	d	15.04.59	Ch Ambassador of Buttonoak	Lucinda of Cheyenne	R I Stewart	Mr & Mrs D A Urquhart	6
1962							
Ch Bulstaff Brobdingnag	d	21.03.59	Ch Ambassador of Buttonoak	Bulstaff Felicity	Mr & Mrs R E Short	Mrs K A Burt	4
Ch Bulstaff Leah	b	20.09.59	Bulstaff Sergeant Major of Parisgarden	Ch Bulstaff Prudence of Torthorwald	Mr & Mrs R E Short	Mrs B Blake	5
Ch Mi Brandy of Marbette	d	30.07.58	Ch Ambassador of Buttonoak	Ch Mi-Choice of Marbette	Mmes E B Millard & M Eaton	J Goad	3
Ch Burghley of Bullturn	d	19.10.59	Brave Boy of Bullturn	Burnisher of Bullturn	Mrs F Turnbull	Breeder	3
Ch Dancer of Oldwell	b	25.10.60	Ch Oldwell Mi-Trooper of Marbette	Dilly of Oldwell	H Colliass	Breeder	14
Ch Bulstaff Achilles	d	02.01.61	Ch Bulstaff Brobdingnag	Bulstaff Ambassadress of Buttonoak	Mr & Mrs R E Short	Breeders	24
1963							
Ch Duchess of Oldwell	b	25.10.60	Ch Oldwell Mi-Trooper of Marbette	Dilly of Oldwell	H Colliass	Breeder	5
Ch Lucinda of Cheyenne	b	05.03.57	Pridsor's Alibi	Wendy of Waygateshaw	Mrs E Smith	R I Stewart	3
Ch Buttonoak Meg of Marbette	b	23.12.59	Master Boy of Marbette	Miss Muffet of Marbette	Mrs M J Kay	Mr & Mrs E L Terry	3
Ch Goodstock Twinkletoes	b	13.10.61	Goodstock Snap Decision	Lady Joyful of Goodstock	Misses E P & L A Goodhall	K Hall	6
1964							
Ch Dandini Prince of Oldwell	d	30.11.61	Ch Mi Brandy of Marbette	Ch Bambino	H Colliass	Breeder	3
Ch Hakmluk of Naukeen	b	14.12.62	Goodstock Bashon	Becky of Tipdixon	G L Blount	Breeder	6
Ch Morejoy Pride Amanda	b	20.12.61	Wyaston Captain Cuttle	Lass of Cleobury	Mrs J James	Breeder	5

Name	Sex	DOB	Sire	Dam	Breeder	Owner	CCs
1965							
Ch Oldwell Toby of Studbergh	d	11.02.62	Ch Master Brandy of Marbette	Miss Polly of Marbette	Mrs D A Butler	H Colliass	4
Ch Miss Oldwell	b	21.05.63	Ch Dandini Prince of Oldwell	Comptessa	Mrs J Morris	H Colliass	5
Ch Jupiter of Sandene	d	09.03.63	Lingmell Thunderstorm	Ch Goodstock Twinkletoes	Mrs P Segar & K Hall	Breeders	4
Ch Regina of Ivywill	b	17.05.58	Rufus of Ivywill	Audrey of Buttonoak	Mr & Mrs E W Leedham	Mrs M Byrnes	3
Ch Goodstock Gay Kavalier	d	10.05.63	Goodstock Bashon	Goodstock Sunshine Girl	Mrs S Saxton	Mr & Mrs C Munday	4
1966							
Ch Taurus of Mureken	d	16.02.64	Ch Bulstaff Achilles	Kirkleatham Joy of Mureken	M & K Gaulton	Mr & Mrs O Davies	6
Ch Trina of Tyffynon	b	07.11.63	Gimingham Check Mate	Morejoy Aureola	F P Festiccio	Breeder	4
Ch Yorkist Minstrel	d	21.12.62	Yorkist Martin	Blonde Nell of Norton	Mrs P Upfold	R C Savage	3
Ch Shabaka of Sandene	d	11.03.64	Lingmell Thunderstorm	Ch Goodstock Twinkletoes	K Hall & Mrs P Segar	Mr & Mrs C Lankester	3
Ch Triumph Herald of Mureken	b	16.02.64	Ch Bulstaff Achilles	Kirkleatham Joy of Mureken	Mr & Mrs K Gaulton	Breeders	3
Ch Goodstock Don Juan	d	02.11.64	Goodstock Sunion	Goodstock Playmate	Misses E P & L A Goodhall	L Hirst & Breeders	4
1967							
Ch Yorkist Magician of Oldwell	d	17.12.64	Ch Oldwell Toby of Studbergh	Yorkist Manetta	Mrs M Reynolds	H Colliass	5
Ch Gimingham Royal Flush	b	16.07.62	Ch Bulstaff Achilles	Gimingham Apeach of Buttonoak	Mrs M Thomas	Mrs M L Elliott	3
Ch Wyaston Tudor Prince	d	20.10.62	Wyaston Captain Cuttle	Wyaston Tudor Lass	D B Oliff	Mr & Mrs A C Clark	3
Ch Morejoy Eastern Princess	b	30.03.65	Gimington Check Mate	Morejoy Captain's Lady	Mrs J James	Breeder	13
Ch Bulstaff Rosalynde	b	10.08.64	Ch Bulstaff Achilles	Ch Regina of Ivywill	M & Mrs R E Short	Mr & Mrs W Leedham	3
Ch Darrell of Kelwall	d	04.02.65	Ch Oldwell Toby of Studbergh	Cortella of Kelwall	Mr & Mrs W Pratt	Breeders	3
Ch Harvester of Lombardy	d	04.09.65	Marci of Lombardy	Gimingham No Trumps	Mrs D Price	Breeder	7
1968							
Little Miss of Oldwell	b	01.06.65	Ch Oldwell Toby of Studbergh	Ch Miss Oldwell	H Colliass	Breeder	8
Ch Mister of Oldwell	d	01.06.65	Ch Oldwell Toby of Studbergh	Ch Miss Oldwell	H Colliass	Breeder	5
Ch Regent of Oldwell	d	21.07.65	Ch Oldwell Toby of Studbergh	Delia of Oldwell	H Colliass	Breeder	4

Name	Sex	DOB	Sire	Dam	Breeder	Owner	CCs
Ch Myrtle of Oldwell	b	27.08.65	Ch Oldwell Toby of Studbergh	Garamond Judy	H Colliass	Breeder	4
Ch Derry of Kelwell	d	19.04.66	Ch Oldwell Toby of Studbergh	Cortell of Kelwall	Mr & Mrs W Pratt	Miss S Howard	4
1969							
Ch Bulstaff Topsy	b	18.02.67	Ch Bulstaff Achilles	Bulstaff Tamsin	Mr & Mrs R E Short	Breeders	6
Ch Showell Zarbor	b	22.01.67	Ch Oldwell Toby of Studbergh	Cortessa of Kelwall	Mr & Mrs D Cook	Breeders	5
Ch Kwintra Tammy of Tyfynnon	b	14.01.67	Terror of Tyfynnon	Goodstock Fantasia	F P Festiccio	Mrs J Clark	6
Ch Oldwell Queen Guenevive of Mureken	b	04.02.67	Ch Dandini Prince of Oldwell	Sherharazade of Mureken	Mr & Mrs K Gaulton	H Colliass	10
1970							
Ch Rommell of Ivywill	d	19.03.67	Ch Oldwell Toby of Studbergh	Ch Bulstaff Rosalynde	Mr & Mrs W Leedham	Breeders	6
Ch Claude of Oldwell	d	28.05.67	Darby of Oldwell	Dotelle of Oldwell	H Colliass	Breeder	7
1971							
Ch Yorkist Maid Marion	b	14.06.68	Defender of Maybrook	Yorkist Manetta	Mrs M Reynolds	H J Lucas	4
Ch Pekingtown Abece	b	06.09.69	Bulstaff Turvey	Bugatti of Overdeben	J Coles	Breeder	19
Ch Pitman's Lady Penelopy of Bullpug	b	18.09.69	Bulstaff Turvey	Lady Cleopatra of Naukeen	J & L Leeson	Mr & Mrs H Burton	3
Ch Bulstaff Revelry	d	14.05.69	Bulstaff Turvey	Bulstaff Jessica	Mr & Mrs R Short	Breeders	3
Ch Pitman's Gentleman Jim	d	18.09.69	Bulstaff Turvey	Lady Cleopatra of Naukeen	J & L Leeson	Breeders	9
1972							
Ch Copperfield Martin Chuzzlewitt	d	26.01.69	Ch Yorkist Magician of Oldwell	Copperfield Alma of Overdeben	Mr & Mrs G Warren	Breeders	3
Ch Pitman's Sir Albert	d	09.12.70	Ch Bulstaff Revelry	Pitman's Lady Dorothea	Mr & Mrs J Leeson	Breeders	9
Ch Thorfin of Oldwell	d	26.08.70	Ch Regent of Oldwell	Camelot of Mureken	Mr & Mrs R Benamore	H Colliass	5
Ch Copperfield Sarah Pocket	b	17.02.70	Ch Yorkist Magician of Oldwell	Copperfield Alma of Overdeben	Mr & Mrs G Warren	Breeders	16
Ch Stephan of Naukeen	d	15.07.69	Ch Claude of Oldwell	Samantha of Naukeen	J P Ramsdale	G L Blount	3
Ch Lombardy Simon of Silverfarm	d	16.07.68	Ch Harvester of Lombardy	Valorous of Lombardy	Mrs L Parkes	Mrs D Price	3
1973							
Ch Lombardy Tristam	d	07.01.71	Ch Lombardy Simon of Silverfarm	Fortun of Lombardy	Mrs D Price	Breeder	12

Name	Sex	DOB	Sire	Dam	Breeder	Owner	CCs
Ch Hannah of Oldwell	b	28.08.70	Ch Regent of Oldwell	Camelot of Mureken	Mr & Mrs R Benamore	H Colliass	3
Ch Showell Yibor	d	15.11.69	Showell Zorba	Showell Dorinda of Kelwall	Mr & Mrs D Cook	Mr & Mrs W Pratt	4
Ch Naukeen Loraine	b	06.01.72	Ch Regent of Oldwell	Ma Bell of Naukeen	G L Blount	Breeder	7
1974							
Ch Doomwatch Gipsy of Oldwell	b	08.09.72	Azer of Oldwell	Ch Yorkist Maid Marion	Mr & Mrs H Lucas	H Colliass	5
Ch Frederick of Kelwall	d	01.05.71	Ch Showell Yibor	Ebony of Kelwall	Mr & Mrs W Pratt	Breeders	11
Ch Bulstaff Heritage of Ellney	d	14.08.70	Ch Bulstaff Revelry	Bulstaff Clodagh	Mr & Mrs R Short	Mrs M Elliott	5
Ch Yorkist Miss Muffet	b	19.10.72	Salvateo Don Sebastian of Jensymon	Yorkist Miss Meryl	Mrs H Reynolds	Breeder	3
Ch Bunsoro Cloudburst	d	31.01.73	Stormcloud of Naukeen	Ubonny Blonde of Bunsoro	Mr & Mrs Harris	Breeders	7
1975							
Ch Leyrigg Rhinestone Ruby	b	17.07.73	Azer of Oldwell	Damaran Aristo Gold	Mr & Mrs S Lowrie	Breeders	12
Ch Nicholas of Oldwell	d	25.12.71	Ch Thorfin of Oldwell	Bridget of Oldwell	H Colliass	Breeder	3
Ch Yorkist Marquis	d	19.10.72	Salvateo Don Sebastian of Jensymon	Yorkist Miss Meryll	Mrs M Reynolds	Mr & Mrs L Hirst	3
Ch Copperfield Ben Allen	d	01.12.73	Maverick of Oldwell of Copperfield	Copperfield Miss Georgiana	Mr & Mrs G Warren	Mr & Mrs W A Wood	11
Ch Doomwatch Miss Fortune of Oldwell	b	08.09.72	Azer of Oldwell	Ch Yorkist Maid Marion	Mr & Mrs H Lucas	H Colliass	5
1976							
Ch Bunsoro Donna	b	09.10.73	Ch Pitman's Gentleman Jim	Bunsoro Bellestarr	Mr & Mrs Harris	Breeders	8
Ch Doomwatch Brigand	d	08.09.72	Azer of Oldwell	Ch Yorkist Maid Mrarion	Mr & Mrs H Lucas	Breeders	3
Ch Bonnie of Kelwall	b	05.04.73	Azer of Oldwell	Ailsa of Kelwall	Mr & Mrs W Pratt	Breeders	4
Ch Scott of Oldwell	d	28.02.74	Azer of Oldwell	Lucky Charm of Ladydale	Mrs Butler	H Colliass	3
Ch Colom Florin	b	10.07.74	Ch Lombardy Simon of Silverfarm	Lombardy Rosamunda	Mrs W Cox	Breeder	5
Ch Craigylea Sir Galahad	d	24.08.74	Ch Pitman's Gentleman Jim	Suttonoak Countess Charmaine	Mr & Mrs W Newton	Breeders	16
Ch Bulstaff Solomon	d	17.01.74	Maverick of Oldwell of Copperfield	Overdeben Cresta	Mrs C Burnham	C Nunn	5
Ch Erazmas of Oldwell	d	14.02.75	Othello of Oldwell	Ch Simbec Clarissa of Oldwell	H Colliass	Breeder	3
Ch Simbec Clarissa of Oldwell	b	29.11.72	Azer of Oldwell	Pitman's Queen	Mr & Mrs Alder	H Colliass	3

Name	Sex	DOB	Sire	Dam	Breeder	Owner	CCs
1977							
Ch Honeybee of Oldwell	b	29.03.75	Ch Nicholas of Oldwell	St Mungo Minerva	Dr & Mrs Fraser	H Colliass	13
Ch Copperfield Samuel Weller	d	03.04.73	Maverick of Oldwell of Copperfield	Copperfield Alma of Overbeden	Mr & Mrs G Warren	Breeders	3
Ch Knightguard Black Douglas	d	01.10.71	Ch Showell Yibor	Showell Talina	Mrs J McKnight	I Maceachern	3
Ch Bunsoro Dianna	b	09.10.73	Ch Pitman's Gentleman Jim	Bunsoro Bellestarr	Mr & Mrs Harris	Breeders	3
1978							
Ch Verona of Oldwell	b	24.07.76	Ch Nicholas of Oldwell	St Mungo Minerva	Dr & Mrs Fraser	H Colliass	11
Ch Pitman's Buccaneer	d	01.09.75	Ch Craigylea Sir Galahad	Pitman's Lady Katharina	Mr & Mrs J Leeson	Breeders	3
Ch Bunsoro Penny Lane	b	05.11.75	Ch Bunsoro Cloudburst	Ubonny Blonde of Bunsoro	Mr & Mrs Harris	Breeders	10
Ch Frazer of Oldwell	d	24.07.76	Ch Nicholas of Oldwell	St Mungo Minerva	Dr & Mrs Fraser	H Colliass	4
Ch Blaze of Oldwell	d	01.02.74	Azer of Oldwell	Copperfield Becky	Mr & Mrs C Munday	Breeders	5
Ch Naukeen Ranger	d	24.10.76	Naukeen Masked Major	Ch Naukeen Loraine	G L Blount	Breeder	3
Ch Naukeen Leila	b	07.05.74	Azer of Oldwell	Ch Naukeen Loraine	G L Blount	Breeder	3
Ch Milbarsa Man Friday of Lystan	d	14.01.77	Ch Yorkist Marquis	Copperfield Flopsom	Miss B Lang & A Milne	F J Attwater	6
1979							
Ch Doomwatch Juanita of Oldwell	b	23.07.76	Ch Scott of Oldwell	Ch Doomwatch Gipsy of Oldwell	H Colliass	Mr & Mrs H Lucas	3
Ch Kracka of Oldwell	d	24.07.76	Ch Nicholas of Oldwell	St Mungo Minerva	Mr & Mrs Fraser	H Colliass	8
Ch Maggie May of Bunsoro	b	07.08.77	Ch Bunsoro Cloudburst	Sackville Princess	T A Massey	Mr & Mrs Harris	11
Ch Lombardy Llewellyn	d	22.11.75	Ch Lombardy Tristam	Lombardy Hermia	Mrs D Price	Breeder	4
Ch Crystal of Oldwell	b	28.02.77	Ch Nicholas of Oldwell	St Mungo Minerva	Mrs Fraser	H Colliass	13
Ch Clyde of Kelwall	d	26.11.76	Ch Frederick of Kelwall	Ch Bonnie of Kelwall	Mr & Mrs W Pratt	Breeders	5
1980							
Ch Copperfield Maria Lobbs	b	01.12.73	Maverick of Oldwell of Copperfield	Copperfield Miss Georgiana	Mr & Mrs G Warren	Breeders	3
Ch Todomas Duchess	b	07.08.77	Ch Bunsoro Cloudburst	Sackville Princess	T A Massey	Breeder	7
Ch Leyrigg Tora Tora	d	13.09.77	Ch Craigylea Sir Galahad	Leyrigg Adela Angelina	Mr & Mrs Lawrie	Mr & Mrs W Tosh	6
Ch Bunsoro Bombadier	d	24.07.78	Ch Bombadillo of Bunsoro	Ch Bunsoro Dianna	Mr & Mrs Harris	Breeders	10
Ch Purston Harvest Gold	d	27.05.77	Ch Frederick of Kelwall	Naukeen Viola	M Collins	Breeder	3
Ch Bombadillo of Bunsoro	d	07.08.77	Ch Bunsoro Cloudburst	Sackville Princess	T A Massey	Mr & Mrs Harris	4
1981							
Ch Bunsoro Proud Mary	b	24.07.78	Ch Bombadillo of Bunsoro	Ch Bunsoro Dianna	Mr & Mrs Harris	R W James	3

Name	Sex	DOB	Sire	Dam	Breeder	Owner	CCs
Ch Bryany Rima Renown	b	08.11.75	Naukeen Black Beauty	Merry Marina of Bryany	C Taylor	Breeder	3
Ch Colom Jumbo	d	16.04.78	Ch Naukeen Ranger	Ch Colom Florin	Mrs W Cox	Breeder	4
Ch Todomas Tamar	b	17.12.79	Ch Bunsoro Bombadier	Delilah of Bunsoro	T A Massey	Breeder	16
Ch Star of Oldwell	b	15.06.77	Ch Nicholas of Oldwell	Rita of Oldwell	Mr & Mrs Smith	H Colliass	4
Ch Yoric of Oldwell	d	24.07.76	Ch Nicholas of Oldwell	St Mungo Minerva	Dr & Mrs Fraser	H Colliass	3
Ch Colom Nelly	b	16.04.78	Ch Naukeen Ranger	Ch Colom Florin	W Cox	Mrs W Cox	4
Ch Daffreda of Kelwall	b	14.12.78	Ch Frederick of Kelwall	Clancy of Kelwall	Mr & Mrs W Pratt	Breeders	3
Ch Pitman's Deputy	d	28.06.78	Ch Pitman's Buccaneer	Naukeen Pepi	Mr & Mrs Leeson	Breeders	4
Ch Todomas Tanya of Bunsoro	b	17.12.79	Ch Bunsoro Bombadier	Delilah of Bunsoro	T A Massey	Mr & Mrs Harris	5
Ch Bunsoro Buzcock	d	10.01.79	Ch Bombadillo of Bunsoro	Ch Bunsoro Donna	Mr & Mrs Harris	J Dixon	3
1982							
Ch Mystro of Oldwell	d	24.05.80	Mascot of Oldwell	Zulu of Oldwell	H Colliass	Breeder	5
Ch Carndearg El Toro de Oro	d	28.06.78	Clyth Fuirbidh	Leontas Beauty's Joy	Mr & Mrs Maceachern	D Hamilton	3
Ch Coombelane River Worle	b	24.08.79	Seafoam Hawk	Coombelane River Effra	Mrs Norman	May	7
Ch Barnaby of Oldwell	d	14.5.77	Mascot of Oldwell	Leta of Oldwell	Miss E Munro	F Pegler	7
Ch Ivywill Wagga Wagga of Colom	b	21.03.81	Dynamic Kid	Colom Dilly of Ivywill	Mr & Mrs Leedham	H Colliass	10
Ch Twynfields Bryden	d	06.07.80	Twynfields Samson	Twynfields Bonny Belinda	GP & M Calverley	Mrs W Cox	3
Ch Leyrigg Maurven Sweet Water	b	28.08.80	Struanmor An Nuna	Leyrigg Silver Jewel	Mr & Mrs Lawrie	Breeders	4
1983							
Ch Leyrigg Major Calum	d	28.08.80	Struanmor An Nuna	Leyrigg Silver Jewel	Mr & Mrs Lawrie	Breeders	3
Ch Jomaro Esta	b	24.03.80	Ch Kracka of Oldwell	Barrus Andromeda	Mrs B Bateman	Breeder	4
Ch Copperfield Sampson	d	22.12.79	Copperfield Henry Warden	Copperfield Betsy White	Mr & Mrs G Warren	Mrs P Jeans-Brown	3
Ch Copperfield Pip	d	08.09.81	Ch Copperfield Sampson	Barloy Ideal Lass	Mr & Mrs G Warren	Breeders	3
Ch Tartuffe Arachne	b	07.12.81	Ch Pitman's Deputy	Whitebarns Pride of Furneux	Mrs S Reynolds	Breeder	4
Ch Seafoam Miranda	b	30.10.81	Ch Craigylea Sir Galahad	Seafoam Naomi	Mrs E Evans	Breeder	5
Ch Lombardy Harvey	d	09.08.79	Ch Lombardy Tristam	Lombardy Hermia	Mrs D Price	Breeder	3
Ch Barrus Beaumont	d	02.06.80	Barrus Advocate	Peggotty of Barrus	Mr & Miss Russell	Breeders	4
1984							
Ch Jagofpeeko Inam of Oldwell	d	26.05.82	Ch Kracka of Oldwell	Gypsy Jag of Peeko	Mr & Mrs E Grant	H Colliass	6
Ch Naukeen Melody of Dreadnot	b	14.09.82	Samuel of Oldwell of Naukeen	Candy of Naukeen	G Blount	M McNaught	6

Name	Sex	DOB	Sire	Dam	Breeder	Owner	CCs
Ch Graecia Centaur	d	14.10.81	Struanmor An Nuna	Batheda of Ellisdene	A B & Mrs Rostron	Breeders	4
Ch Naukeen Daniel	d	07.11.80	Samuel of Oldwell of Naukeen	Naukeen Racheal	G Blount	Breeder	3
Ch Naukeen Major Kew of Eastlynn	d	22.06.83	Ch Naukeen Ranger	Naukeen Toni	G Blount	Mrs M Qualters	16
Ch Linzie of Oldwell	b	12.10.82	Ch Frazer of Oldwell	Kizzie Conundrum	Mr & Mrs Kiesslinger	H Colliass	5
Ch Coldstream of Bunsoro	d	25.04.82	Ch Bombadillo of Bunsoro	Petabrook Kirsty	Mrs Z King	F E Simpson	4
1985							
Ch Sharwell's Mean Mr Mustard of Pitman's	d	10.05.83	Ch Pitman's Deputy	Lady Kate of Recnard at Sharwell	Mr & Mrs K Bakewell	Mr & Mrs Leeson	12
Ch Saphire of Oldwell	b	23.11.80	Clywoods Red Baron of Oldwell	Ch Honeybee of Oldwell	H Colliass	Breeder	3
Ch Zeela of Oldwell	b	24.05.80	Mascot of Oldwell	Zulu of Oldwell	H Colliass	Breeder	3
Ch Wyburn Tarna	b	30.03.84	Quarto of Oldwell	Wyburn Kia La	Miss C Ridsdale	Breeder	3
Ch Sylvia of Oldwell	b	13.10.83	Ch Kracka of Oldwell	Gypsy Jag of Peeko	Mr & Mrs E Grant	H Colliass	3
Ch Mystic of Oldwell	d	19.10.82	Clywoods Red Baron of Oldwell	Naukeen Wynne	Mrs M Keely	H Colliass	3
Ch Jagofpeeko Inara	b	26.05.82	Ch Kracka of Oldwell	Gypsy Jag of Peeko	Mr & Mrs E Grant	Breeders	3
Ch Wyburn Rula of Oldwell	d	15.07.82	Porthos of Oldwell	Wyburn Becca	Miss C Ridsdale	H Colliass	6
Ch Jostmaro Mascorade of Oldwell	b	04.08.83	Ch Barnaby of Oldwell	Ch Jostmaro Esta	Mrs B Bateman	H Colliass	4
Ch Tartuffe Apollo	d	01.12.81	Ch Pitman's Deputy	Whitebarns Pride of Furneux	Mrs S Reynolds	Breeder	4
1986							
Ch Bullrolyn Bonny Lass	b	16.09.82	Dynamic Kid	Friendly Lass	Mr & Mrs Kennedy	D Brown	3
Ch Rythm of Oldwell	b	02.05.84	Ch Mystro of Oldwell	Ch Jagofpeeko Inara	Mr & Mrs E Grant	H Colliass	4
Ch Celeste of Graecia	b	02.06.84	Ch Graecia Centaur	Conireed Elsa	Mrs C Alcock	Mr & Mrs Rostron	8
Ch Todomas Anselm	d	23.07.82	Ch Bunsoro Bombadier	Ch Todomas Duchess	T Massey	Breeder	3
Ch Bryany Brunette	b	24.11.83	Ch Leyrigg Major Callum	Red Hunter of Bryany	C Taylor	Capt, Mrs & Ms Goodlad	4
Ch Jagofpeeko Boadicea	b	02.05.84	Ch Mystro of Oldwell	Ch Jagofpeeko Inara	Mr & Mrs E Grant	E Grant	6
1987							
Ch Cadenham Davrian	d	23.09.81	Ch Clyde of Kelwall	Coombelane River Effra	Miss Pegler	Breeder	3
Ch Bold Borage Jagofpeeko	d	06.05.85	Jostmaro Clarance of Oldwell	Oldwell Tara	Mrs P James	E Grant	9
Ch Tartuffe Priam	b	14.08.81	Ch Pitman's Deputy	Micglen Tupny Button	Mrs S Reynolds	Breeder	3
Ch Naukeen Thunder	d	31.10.81	Samuel of Oldwell of Naukeen	Candy of Naukeen	G L Blount	Breeder	3
Ch Gosscroft Special Lady	b	17.08.84	Ch Mystro of Oldwell	Smashing Lady of Gosscroft	Mrs M Turner	H Colliass	3

Name	Sex	DOB	Sire	Dam	Breeder	Owner	CCs
of Oldwell							
Ch Cadenham Ben Gunn	d	29.07.85	Ch Oldwell Corrallian	Cadenham Chance Meeting	Mmes Wilson & Pegler	Mrs F Wilson	6
Ch Bartoy Nice One	b	12.05.85	Ch Mystic of Oldwell	Barloy Hebreena	Mrs B Browning	Breeder	3
Ch Maxstoke Bassey	b	07.06.85	Colom Dubbo	Newton Nina	Mr & Mrs Jones	Breeders	6
1988							
Ch Galastock Danny Boy	d	05.03.86	Ch Sharwell's Mean Mr Mustard of Pitman's	Victoria of Galastock	Mr & Mrs Newton	Breeders	18
Ch Millie of Pitman's	b	04.09.85	Ch Sharwell's Mean Mr Mustard of Pitman's	Recnad Glint of Gold	J Partridge	Miss J Jones	3
Ch Bryany Bullette	b	24.11.83	Ch Leyrigg Major Callum	Red Hunter of Bryany	C Taylor	Breeder	3
Ch Oldwell Carmen	b	10.08.86	Jostmaro Clarance of Oldwell	Oldwell Fayette	H Colliass	Breeder	4
Ch Oldwell Corrallian	d	01.06.83	Ch Barnaby of Oldwell	Ch Star of Oldwell	H Colliass	Mrs P Brittle	3
Ch Galastock Sugar and Spice	b	05.03.86	Ch Sharwell's Mean Mr Mustard of Pitman's	Victoria of Galastock	Mr & Mrs Newton	C Newton & Ms L Millward	10
Ch Jazzy Jaffa	d	09.12.85	Spartan General of Salches	Cherry Pit Girl	D Roscoe	Mr & Mrs James	3
Ch Lady Marona of Pitman's	b	06.02.86	Ch Sharwell's Mean Mr Mustard of Pitman's	Madam Fee-Fee of Leyrigg	Mr & Mrs Lowrie	Mr & Mrs Leeson	4
Ch Salches Ceana Doublet	b	16.04.86	Graecia Magician	Elkin Candida of Salches	Mr & Mrs Barber	Breeders	5
Ch Wyburn Rhian of Oldwell	d	30.09.83	Porthos of Oldwell	Wyburn Becca	Miss C Ridsdale	H Colliass	3
1989							
Ch Oldwell Kalif	d	10.08.86	Jostmaro Clarance of Oldwell	Oldwell Fayette	H Colliass	Breeder	5
Ch Saturn of Graecia	d	07.07.87	Ch Craecia Centaur	Wilward Naughty Nina	K Rostron	Mr & Mrs Rostron	5
Ch Dreadnot Melody Maker	b	10.10.86	Hrothgar of Tartuffe	Ch Naukeen Melody of Dreadnot	Mrs M McNaught	Breeder	6
Ch Leyrigg French Pickle of Meitza	d	06.02.86	Ch Sharwell's Mean Mr Mustard of Pitman's	Madam Fee Fee of Leyrigg	Mr & Mrs Lowrie	Miss F Miller	4
Ch Maxstoke Elkie	b	18.05.87	Ch Bold Borage Jagofpeeko	Maxstoke Cleopatra	Mr & Mrs Jones	Breeders	5
Ch Boomerang of Naukeen	d	30.11.84	Naukeen Marksman	Eastlynn Annie-Jean	Mrs M Qualters	G Blount	3
Ch Todomas Ingrid of Bunsoro	b	25.09.87	Ch Todomas Anselm	Princess Teela Aleet	T Massey	Mr & Mrs Harris	3
Ch Banshee of Bunsoro	b	28.06.88	Bosun of Bunsoro	Maymar Lady Be Good	Mrs K Farley	Mr & Mrs Harris	5
Ch Oldwell Rayna	b	25.07.86	Ch Wyburn Rula of Oldwell	Ch Sylva of Oldwell	H Colliass	Breeder	4
Ch Norwegian Wood of Rodekes	d	20.06.87	Ch Sharwell Mean Mr Mustard of Pitman's	Belvedere Belle	Mrs R Higginson	Mr & Mrs Higginson	13
Ch Bostrom Amanda's Dream	b	21.10.86	Gemtor King Benjiman	Bulltzar's Hera of Bostrom	Mr, Mrs & Miss Hay	Breeders	3

Name	Sex	DOB	Sire	Dam	Breeder	Owner	CCs
1990							
Ch Gemtor Frieda Frauline of Bostrom	b	28.09.85	Taybank Tartar of Bultzar	Caiterlee Angelina of Gemtor	Mr & Mrs Marshall	Mr, Mrs & Miss Kay	3
Ch Sylou Startrekker	d	11.12.88	Ch Saturn of Graecia	Zara Lady Luck	Mr & Mrs Parry	Breeders	8
Ch Twynfields Eleazar	d	10.02.80	Twynfields Titus The King	Twynfields Gemina	Mr & Mrs Calverley	Mrs B Sutcliffe	3
Ch Todomas Kathryn	b	19.11.87	Bronson of Bunsoro at Todomas	Todomas Theresa	T Massey	R McKenzie	3
Ch Oldwell Saxon of Bournevalley	d	31.05.88	Oldwell Oscar	Tamara of Oldwell	M Ingram	Mr & Mrs Bowman	6
Ch Graecia Celestine	b	24.08.88	Ch Galastock Danny Boy	Ch Celeste of Graecia	Mr & Mrs Rostron	Breeders	4
Ch Oldwell Saint	d	02.03.87	Oldwell Oscar	Ch Sylva of Oldwell	H Colliass	Breeder	3
Ch Bryany Claudette	b	10.01.89	Ch Leyrigg French Pickle of Meitza	Ch Bryany Bullette	C Taylor	Breeder	5
Ch Oldwell Isla	b	24.04.88	Ch Jagotpeeko Inam of Oldwell	Ch Sylva of Oldwell	H Colliass	Breeder	3
1991							
Ch Dark Prince of Pitman's	d	24.07.88	Ch Sharwells Mean Mr Mustard of Pitman's	Emreds Sweet Surprise	J Brassington	Mr, Mrs & Miss Leeson	5
Ch Maxstoke Bold Herbie Jagotpeeko	d	18.05.87	Ch Bold Borage Jagotpeeko	Maxstoke Cleopatra	Mr & Mrs Jones	E Grant	6
Ch Careless Whisper of Meitzad	b	06.02.86	Ch Sharwell's Mean Mr Mustard of Pitman's	Madam Fee-Fee of Leyrigg	Mr & Mrs Lowrie	Miss F Miller	3
Ch Todomas Yvonne	b	22.02.89	Ch Todomas Anselm	Todomas Zena	A Massey	Breeder	4
Ch Oldwell Morven	b	24.04.88	Ch Jagotpeeko Inam of Oldwell	Ch Sylva of Oldwell	H Colliass	Breeder	4
Ch Oldwell Trumps	d	10.10.89	Oldwell Oscar	Ch Oldwell Carmen	H Colliass	Breeder	7
Ch Patchings August Lady	b	02.08.88	Pitman's Major	Maggie of Pitman's	Mrs L Wade	Breeder	3
Ch Beltarn Simba at Zarrott	d	21.03.89	Ch Galastock Danny Boy	Beltarn Sea Breeze	D Hadwen	Mr & Mrs Evans	3
1992							
Ch Jusamo Lucifer	d	05.10.85	Tadyboi Bilbo Baggins	Missie Mischief of Jusamo	Mr & Mrs Collins	Mr Pickhaver & Mrs P Snell	3
Ch Lepsco Lady Elise of Flintstock	b	31.03.90	Dajean Our Man Flint	Maxstoke Meggie	W Scott	Mr & Mrs Gunn	6
Ch Tyleoni Kiss the Bride	b	23.12.89	The Brigadier From Tartuffe	Nightwatch Dawn Gossamer of Tyleoni	Mrs J Robison	Mr & Mrs Davies	4
Ch Dajean Golddust	b	15.11.90	Ch Saturn of Graecia	Dajean Golden Autocrat	Miss S Wood	Mr & Mrs Ling	21

The Poachers Foe

Name	Sex	DOB	Sire	Dam	Breeder	Owner	CCs
Ch Naukeen Night Ranger	d	29.12.89	Maxstoke Tegwyn	Naukeen Enchantress	G Blount	Breeder	3
Ch Jagofpeeko Wood Sorrel	d	15.06.89	Ch Maxstoke Bold Herbie Jagofpeeko	Ch Jagofpeeko Boadicea	E Grant	Breeder	7
Ch Morvern Elyse	b	28.10.89	Bronson of Bunsoro at Todomas	Morvern Dulcie	Mr & Mrs McInnes	Breeders	3
1993							
Ch Bryany Starboy	d	10.01.89	Ch Leyrigg French Pickle of Meitza	Ch Bryany Bullette	C Taylor	Breeder	3
Ch Galastock Sorceress	b	14.11.90	Galastock Mister Todd	Graecia Sunglow of Galastock	Mrs J Townsend	Breeder	4
Ch Dajean Red Dragon	d	15.11.90	Ch Saturn of Graecia	Dajean Golden Autocrat	Miss S Wood	G Slater & Miss T Jukes	17
Ch Filand Man of Harlech at Cadenham	d	29.08.90	Ch Cadenham Benn Gunn	Founder of Filand	Miss S Webley	Mmes F Wilson & D Pegler	4
Ch Todomas Tamara	b	30.12.89	Todomas Igor	Todomas Jemima	T Massey	Breeder	3
Ch Raflyn Sweet Savanna	b	03.09.90	Ch Boomerang of Naukeen	Raflyn Sweet Tamarisk	Mr & Mrs Wykes	Breeders	3
Ch Naukeen Heath Thyme	d	26.10.90	Naukeen Rambler	Bo Peep for Naukeen	G Blount	Breeder	3
Ch Murbisa The Ferryman	d	14.08.89	Bosun of Bunsoro	Murbisa Scarlet Ribbons	Mrs M Day	Breeder	3
Ch Pitman's Classic Lady	b	14.04.91	Pitman's Bonaparte	Jobull's Julie	Mssrs & Mrs Leeson	Breeders	3
Ch Maxstoke Einwyn	d	30.08.89	Maxstoke Tegwyn	Ch Maxstoke Elkie	Mr & Mrs Jones	A Loughan	4
Ch Blazin's Jubullation of Jobull	b	05.02.92	Am Ch Blazin's Studz McKenzie	Am Ch Sojourner Queen of Soul	Mr & Mrs Lapaglia	Miss J Jones	7
Ch Murbisa Spring Tides at Rossir	b	14.08.89	Bosun of Bunsoro	Murbisa Scarlet Ribbons	Mrs M Day	Mrs A Hannay	3
1994							
Ch Bryany Bronyia	b	10.10.89	Ch Leyrigg French Pickle of Meitza	Ch Bryany Bullette	C Taylor	Breeder	3
Ch Rakwana Oberon of Tartuffe	d	10.05.89	The Brigadier from Tartuffe	Nightwatch Midnight Star	Mrs G Chapple	Mrs S Reynolds	3
Ch Brinscall Barnaby	d	12.12.90	Ch Graecia Centaur	Gilcliffe Daisy of Brinscall	Mrs L Crowley	Breeder	3
Ch Fantasy Girl	b	12.10.90	Ch Dark Prince of Pitman's	Ch Todomas Kathryn	R McKenzie	Breeder	3
Ch Cadenham Blonde Ambition	b	08.11.92	Ch Oldwell Saxon of Bournevalley	Dolly Daydream of Cadenham	Mmes A Wilson & D Pegler	Mr & Mrs J Seger	10
Ch Naukeen Morag of Dreadnot	b	26.10.90	Naukeen Rambler	Bo Peep for Naukeen	G Blount	Mrs M McNaught	3
Ch Todomas Madoc	d	11.10.91	Ch Dark Prince of Pitman's	Todomas Yelda	T Massey	Breeder	3
Ch Iron Bru of Evenstar	d	17.04.91	Iron King of Evenstar	Persian Dawn	S Copp	Mr & Mrs Webster	3

Name	Sex	DOB	Sire	Dam	Breeder	Owner	CCs
Ch Cadenham Cherokee at Bournevalley	b	08.11.92	Ch Oldwell Saxon of Bournevalley	Dolly Daydream of Cadenham	Mmes A Wilson & D Pegler	Mr & Mrs A Bowman	4
Ch Todomas Naomi	b	05.12.91	Todomas Igor	Todomas Jemima	T Massey	Breeder	3
Ch Jamemos Pay Homage to Carl	d	08.80.91	Jamemos Bo Jangles	Rosita of Graecia	Mr & Mrs W James	Mrs M Tonge	4

1995

Name	Sex	DOB	Sire	Dam	Breeder	Owner	CCs
Ch Licassa Jolly Roger	d	26.01.93	Ch Oldwell Saint	Licassa Lady Rogina	B Blunden & C Quantrill	Breeders	3
Ch Morvern Grenadier	d	03.02.93	Ch Todomas Madoc	Ch Morvern Elyse	Mr & Mrs McInnes	Breeders	3
Ch Copperfield Capt Bailey	d	31.10.91	Ch Dark Prince of Pitman's	Salches Tirana Regent of Copperfield	G Warren	Breeder	3
Ch Bournevalley Misty at Meitza	b	12.06.93	Bournevalley's Conan	Bournevalley's Freya	Mr & Mrs A Bowman	Miss F Miller & Mrs M Lander	4
Ch Eastlynn Victoria to Taurleone	b	23.03.92	Ch Boomerang of Naukeen	Naukeen Ballad to Eastlynn	Mrs M Qualters	Mrs O Fowler	3
Ch Bunsoro Red Sails	d	16.11.93	Kingsreach The Navigator of Murbisa	Jamemos Birita of Bunsoro	Mr & Mrs Harris	Breeders	3
Ch Voncalin Night Moves	b	05.05.93	Striped Crusader	Voncalin Lady Double Dealer	Mr & Mrs Wray	Breeders	3
Ch Graecia Mercury	d	16.06.92	Ch Saturn of Graecia	Graecia Gemini	Mr & Mrs Rostron	Breeders	4
Ch Maxstoke Monty	d	28.01.94	Ch Naukeen Heath Thyme	Maxstoke Cyriad	Mr & Mrs Jones	Breeders	5
Ch Hurry v Frankental of Jobull	d	08.08.92	Mercedes Jackadandy	Ebony Face v Frankental	K Arnold	Miss J Jones & Breeder	3

SOME IMPORTANT PEDIGREES

Bluff: first American registered brindle Bullmastiff

Parents	Grandparents	G. Grandparents
SIRE: Mackwyn Excelsior	SIRE: Major of Kalka	SIRE: Tiger Torus
		DAM: Helen
	DAM: Lady of Kalka	SIRE: Joker
		DAM: Cloud Side Dolly
DAM: Woodacre Stormer	SIRE: Sans Faut	SIRE: Bullers Fidelity
		DAM: Wingates Pride
	DAM: Woodacre Terra	SIRE: Farcroft Formative
		DAM: Joy

Farcroft Silvo: first ever Bullmastiff Champion (UK)

Parents	Grandparents
SIRE: Hamil Grip	SIRE: Hamil Terror
	DAM: Hamil Lady
DAM: Farcroft Belltong	SIRE: Farcroft Valiant
	DAM: Farcroft Gallant

Fascination of Felons Fear: first ever American registered Bullmastiff (fawn)

Parents	Grandparents	G. Grandparents	G.G. Grandparents
SIRE Farcroft Felons Frayeur	SIRE Farcroft Faction	SIRE Hamil Halberd	SIRE Hamil Hercules
			DAM Farcroft Crystal
		DAM Farcroft Ferox	SIRE Hamil Grip
			DAM Farcroft Belltong
	DAM Farcroft Fend	SIRE Farcroft Formidable	SIRE Farcroft Agrippa
			DAM Farcroft Repulse
		DAM Farcroft Crystal	SIRE Farcroft Pedro
			DAM Farcroft Agate
DAM Farcroft Fortitude	SIRE Farcroft Finality	SIRE Farcroft Fidelity's Filius	SIRE Farcroft Fidelity
			DAM Farcroft Sleuth
		DAM Farcroft Fealty	SIRE Farcroft Fascist
			DAM Farcroft Tracker
	DAM Farcroft Silvo	SIRE Hamil Grip	SIRE Hamil Terror
			DAM Hamil Lady
		DAM Farcroft Belltong	SIRE Farcroft Valiant
			DAM Farcroft Gallant

Heatherbelle Emperor: first Canadian Champion

Parents	Grandparents	G. Grandparents	G.G. Grandparents
SIRE Pride of Elgin	**SIRE** Bluff	**SIRE** Mackwyn Excelsior	**SIRE** Major Kalka
			DAM Lady of Kalka
		DAM Woodacre Stormer	**SIRE** Sans Faut
			DAM Woodacre Terra
	DAM Farvale Sentinel	**SIRE** Bluff	**SIRE** Mackwyn Excelsior
			DAM Woodacre Stormer
		DAM Rhodenhurst Ruby	**SIRE** Phantom of Crestwood
			DAM Patricia of Crestwood
DAM Harbex Duchess	**SIRE** Toby of Le Tasyll	**SIRE** Fawn Prince	**SIRE** Sans Faut
			DAM May's Pride
		DAM Tigers Repeater	**SIRE** Tiger Superb
			DAM Veronica of Crestwood
	DAM Fairhazel Jenny	**SIRE** Peter Bighead	**SIRE** Phantom of Crestwood
			DAM Phantom Princess of Crestwood
		DAM Shy Girl	**SIRE** Grenadier Brutus
			DAM Prudence of Crestwood

Jeanette of Brooklands of Felons Fear: first American Champion

Parents	Grandparents	G. Grandparents	G.G. Grandparents
SIRE Roger of the Fenns	**SIRE** Don Juan	**SIRE** Farcroft Fascist	**SIRE** Farcroft Fidelity
			DAM Farcroft Crystal
		DAM Pride O'Birches Head	**SIRE** Tiger Torus
			DAM Princess Poppy
	DAM Luzlow Princess	**SIRE** Tiger Prince	**SIRE** Tiger Torus
			DAM Pridzor Belle
		DAM Pridzor Princess	**SIRE** Hamil Halberd
			DAM Farcroft Ferox
DAM Bubbles	**SIRE** Farcroft Felons Frayeur	**SIRE** Farcroft Faction	**SIRE** Farcroft Formidable
			DAM Farcroft Crystal
		DAM Farcroft Fend	**SIRE** Farcroft Fidelity
			DAM Farcroft Sleuth
	DAM Lady Betty of Bowdencourt	**SIRE** Farcroft Fidelity's Filius	**SIRE**
			DAM
		DAM Farcroft Filia Typhoon	**SIRE**
			DAM

Neil: first American registered red Bullmastiff

Parents	Grandparents	G. Grandparents	G.G. Grandparents
SIRE Simba	**SIRE** Athos	**SIRE** Farcroft Fidelity	**SIRE** Shireland Vindictive
			DAM Farcroft Faithful
		DAM Noble	**SIRE**
			DAM
	DAM Lady Athena	**SIRE** Tiger Prince	**SIRE** Tiger Torus
			DAM Princess Poppy
		DAM Pridzor Princess	**SIRE** Tiger Torus
			DAM Pridzor Belle
DAM Freya of Germains	**SIRE** Phantom of Crestwood	**SIRE** Cress	**SIRE**
			DAM
		DAM Tiger Princess	**SIRE**
			DAM
	DAM Beauty's Daughter	**SIRE** Don Juan	**SIRE** Farcroft Fascist
			DAM Pride O' Birches Head
		DAM Princess Beauty	**SIRE**
			DAM

FURTHER READING

Research

Canadian Kennel Club Research and Archives.
American Kennel Club Archives.
Standard Publications of Kennel Clubs in: Australia, Britain, Canada, New Zealand, South Africa, United States of America.
Reminiscence by Mrs D Daniell-Jenkins.
Pioneers by Helma Weeks.
British research by Lyn Pratt with contributions by Mr H E Price (Lombardy) and Dr Desirée Scott.

Graphics

Original graphics by Brigitte Walkey; post production enhancements by Dan Lish, TFH.

Books about the Breed

Hubbard, Clifford L B (1957) *The Bullmastiff,* London: Nicholson & Watson.
Oliff, Douglas B (1988) *The Mastiff and Bullmastiff handbook,* New York: Howell Book House.
Prescott, Mary (1964) *How to raise and train a Bullmastiff,* New Jersey: TFH Publications.
Prescott, Mary (1989) *Bullmastiffs,* New Jersey: TFH Publications.
Pratt, Lyn (1996) *Bullmastiffs Today,* Lydney: Ringpress.

Training Information

Burke, Lew (1976) *Lew Burke's dog training,* New Jersey: TFH Publications.
Handler, Barbara S (1984) *Best foot forward,* Loveland, Colorado: Alpine Publications.
Koehler, William (1962) *Koehler method of dog training,* New York: Howell Book House.
Maller, Dick and Feinman, Jeffrey (1979) *21 days to a trained dog,* New York: Simon and Schuster.
Mclennan, Bardi (1990) *The canine consultant – audio tape,* Connecticut: Bardwyn Productions Inc, Box 5044, Westport.
Nicholls, Virginia Tuck (1969, 1976) *How to show your own dog,* TFH Publications.
Nicholas, Anne Katherine (1970, 1979, 1989) *The Nicholas guide to dog judging,* New York: Howell Book House.

Other Reading

Fox, M W, B Vet Med, MRCVS (1965, 1972) *Canine behaviour,* Illinois: Charles C Thomas.
Frankling, Eleanor, MA, LRCP, MRCPS (1977) *Practical Dog Breeding and Genetics,* New York: Arco Publications.
Graham, Capt R Portman, LDS, RCS *The mating and whelping of dogs,* London: Popular Dogs Publishing Co, 1954–1969.
Holst, Phyllis A, DVM (1985) *Canine reproduction,* Loveland, Colorado: Alpine Publications.
Hutt, Frederick B (1979) *Genetics for dog breeders,* San Francisco: W H Freeman & Co.
Scott, John Paul and Fuller, John L (1965,1971) *Genetics and the social behaviour of the dog,* Chicago and London: Popular Dogs Publishing Co.

GLOSSARY

angulation: the angles formed by a meeting of the bones, mainly the shoulder and upper arm, stifle and hock.

apple head: rounder head, shaped like an apple.

Best in Show (BIS): a dog show award to the dog judged best of all the breeds.

Best of Breed (BOB): a dog show award to the dog that has defeated all class dogs in its breed.

Best Puppy in Group (BPIG): a dog show award to the puppy that has defeated every puppy in its group.

bailiff: agent or land-steward.

brindle: striped coat effect caused by mixture of black hairs on lighter coloured base.

brisket: the forepart of the body below the chest between the forelegs, closest to the ribs.

burr: inside of the ear, the irregular formation visible within the cup.

Celt: early Briton.

Challenge Certificate (CC): a dog show award in Great Britain. Three, each awarded by a different judge, are required for the dog to qualify as a Champion. CCs are awarded to the Best Dog and Best Bitch at the major (Championship) shows in Great Britain provided the standard is sufficiently high.

Champion (Ch): a prefix used with the name of a show dog that has been recorded a champion by fulfilling the criteria laid down by its national kennel club. (For Great Britain, see above.)

chest: the part of the body or trunk that is enclosed by the ribs.

Companion Dog (CD): a suffix used in North America with the name of a dog that has been recorded a Companion Dog by the national kennel club as a result of having won certain minimum scores in Novice Classes at a specified number of obedience trials licensed by the national kennel club.

Left: Blandford Isha of Gamekeeper.

Ch Nightbeauty Benson Lee. Photo by Animal Pics.

Companion Dog Excellent (CDX): a suffix used in North America with the name of a dog that has been recorded as a Companion Dog Excellent by the national kennel club. It must have obtained certain minimum scores in Open Classes at a specified number of obedience trials licensed by the national kennel club.

cow hocked: when the hocks turn towards each other.

crabbing: dog moves his body at an angle to the line of travel. Also referred to as 'sidewinding', 'sidewheeling', or 'yawing'.

croup: section from hip bones to tail set.

dam: the female parent.

dew claw: an extra claw or functionless digit on the inside of the leg; a rudimentary fifth toe.

dewlap: loose, pendulous skin under the throat.

disqualification: a decision made by a judge following a determination that a dog has a condition that makes it ineligible for any further competition under the dog show rules or under the standard for its breed.

dog: a male dog; also used collectively to designate both male and female.

down in pastern: weak or faulty pastern set at a pronounced angle from the vertical. Sometimes called a slack pastern.

DNA: molecular structure that determines genetic characteristics of living things.

elbow: the joint between the upper arm and the forearm.

even bite: meeting of front teeth at edges with no overlap of upper or lower teeth.

expression: the general appearance of all features of the head as viewed from the front and as typical to the breed.

fancier: a person especially interested and usually active in some phase of the sport of pure-bred dogs.

feet east and west: the toes turned out.

flank: the side of the body between the last rib and the hip.

flews: upper lips pendulous, particularly at their inner corners.

forearm: the bone of the foreleg between the elbow and the pastern.

Wodan Van't Kanterke.

Super Queen of Gamekeeper.

gait: the manner in which a dog walks, trots, or runs; also movement.

haw: a third eyelid or membrane in the inside corner of the eye.

hock: the tarsus or collection of bones of the hind leg forming the joint between the second thigh and the metatarsus; the dog's true heel.

hound glove: rubber glove used on hound coats.

humerus: upper arm or foreleg.

in breeding: the mating of very closely related dogs.

Int: International.

leather: the flap of the ear.

line breeding: the mating of related dogs of the same breed, especially the mating of the dog to one of its ancestors, for example, a dog to his grandam or a bitch to her grandsire.

liver: a colour; deep, reddish brown.

loin: region of the body on either side of the vertebral column between the last ribs and the hindquarters.

mask: dark shading on the foreface.

muzzle: the head in front of the eyes – nasal bone, nostrils, and jaws; foreface.

occiput: upper, back point of the skull.

oestrus: the period during which the bitch is ready to accept the dog for mating.

out at elbow: elbows turning out from the body as opposed to being held close.

out at shoulder: with shoulder blades loosely attached to the body, leaving the shoulders jutting out in relief and increasing the breadth of the front.

outcrossing: the mating of unrelated individuals of the same breed.

overshot: the front teeth (incisors) of the upper jaw overlap and do not touch the front teeth of the lower jaw when the mouth is closed.

pastern: leg below the knee of the front leg or below the hock of the hind leg.

Register of Merit: an award recognised in the USA for a dog that has produced three male champions or four female champions.

roach back: a convex curvature of the back towards the loin.

scissor bite: a bite in which the outer side of the lower incisors touches the inner side of the upper incisors.

second thigh: that part of the hindquarter from the stifle to the hock; lower thigh.

shoulder height: height of the dog's body as measured from the shoulder to the ground.

sickle hocked: inability to straighten the hock joint on the back reach of the hind leg. Also hocks too bent, shaped like a sickle.

single tracking: all footprints falling on a single line of travel. When a dog breaks into a trot, his body is supported by only two legs at a time which move as alternating diagonal pairs. To achieve balance, his legs angle towards a centre line beneath his body, and the greater the speed, the closer they come to tracking in a single line.

sire: the male parent.

slicker brush: brush with teeth of fine, curved wire.

tartar: dark yellow/brown residue on teeth that contributes to gum disease.

topline: the dog's outline from just behind the withers to the tail set.

undershot: the front teeth (incisors) of the lower jaw overlapping or projecting beyond the front teeth of the upper jaw when the mouth is closed.

upper arm: the humerus or bone of the foreleg, between the shoulder blade and the forearm.

vulva: female genital opening to the vagina.

whelps: unweaned puppies.

Winners: an award given at dog shows in North America to the Best Dog (Winners Dog) and the Best Bitch (Winners Bitch) competing in regular classes.

withers: the peak of the dorsal vertebrae; the highest part of the body just behind the neck and between the shoulders.

wrinkle: loose, folding skin on forehead and foreface.

Ch Kimken Shea of Starvalley.

Ch Leatherneck's Gift of Gab, CGC, TDI, the Ranah foundation brood bitch. Owned by Randy and Angie Reese.

Can Ch Shayla's Vigilante O' Banbury.

INDEX